Pollution

The Reference Shelf
Volume 92 • Number 5
H.W. Wilson
A Division of EBSCO Information Services, Inc.

Published by
GREY HOUSE PUBLISHING
Amenia, New York
2020

The Reference Shelf

The books in this series contain reprints of articles, excerpts from books, addresses on current issues, and studies of social trends in the United States and other countries. There are six separately bound numbers in each volume, all of which are usually published in the same calendar year. Numbers one through five are each devoted to a single subject, providing background information and discussion from various points of view and concluding with an index and comprehensive bibliography that lists books, pamphlets, and articles on the subject. The final number of each volume is a collection of recent speeches. Books in the series may be purchased individually or on subscription.

Publisher's Cataloging-In-Publication Data
(Prepared by The Donohue Group, Inc.)

Names: Grey House Publishing, Inc., compiler.
Title: Pollution / [compiled by Grey House Publishing].
Other Titles: Reference shelf ; v. 92, no. 5.
Description: Amenia, New York : Grey House Publishing, 2020. | Includes bibliographical references and index.
Identifiers: ISBN 9781642656046 (v. 92, no. 5) | ISBN 9781642655995 (volume set)
Subjects: LCSH: Pollution. | Refuse and refuse disposal. | Climatic changes. | Environmental policy. | LCGFT: Reference works.
Classification: LCC TD174 .P65 2020 | DDC 363.73--dc23

Printed in Canada

The
Reference Shelf®

Contents

3

4

5

Preface

The Dirty Earth

The development of civilization has been a messy business. Humanity has cleared forests and burned jungles, drained wetlands and dammed rivers, leaving a path of destruction in its wake. The byproduct of humanity's advance is pollution, the introduction of poisonous or harmful substances or objects into the natural environment. Industrial manufacturing and production greatly intensified pollution levels, leaving the world in the twenty-first century to struggle with this destructive legacy. Pollution has destroyed natural ecosystems, and in the process become a threat to humans as physicians have linked hundreds of different health issues to environmental pollutants. With human health and welfare at stake, as well as the current and future sustainability of the planet, pollution ranks as among the most important issues to be faced to ensure a future for generations to come.

The Plasticized World

At the heart of the pollution issue is humanity's search to advance native human capabilities and the functionality of naturally occurring substances. Perhaps no single innovation captures this as well as the invention and spread of plastic. The term "plastic" is derived from the Greek term *plassein*, which means to mold or shape something. Plastics are, at the most basic level, a series of artificial molecules that can be fashioned into materials that can then be shaped and molded. Plastic is ultimately derived from naturally occurring rubber, which is produced by a type of tree that grows in the Amazon basin, first brought to the attention of the Western world by French explorer Charles-Marie de La Condamine. Rubber evolved to protect the rubber tree from damage by plugging holes made by animals in the tree's bark, preventing the loss of moisture and nutrients. Rubber was a revolutionary discovery, leading to the development of rubber tires (notably) in addition to many other objects. But the molecules that give rubber its sticky, moldable properties are found in many other places besides the Amazon basin. Cellulose is a polymer, a chain of repetitive molecules, that occurs naturally in the tissues of trees and plants and is largely responsible for their ability to bend without breaking. Cellulose is also the material that makes the manufacture of paper possible, as long strands can be separated from wood through a process called "pulpin," and then be used to provide strength to a sheet of paper.

Cellulose inspired the first human-made plastic, a material called "Parkesine" created by British inventor Alexander Parkes, who displayed his new invention at the 1862 London International Exhibition. Parkes went bankrupt, but his idea was stolen by two American brothers, John Walsh Hyatt and Isaiah Hyatt, who found a way to make Parkesine more malleable through the addition of camphor. The Hyatt brothers renamed their pilfered product "celluloid" and revealed it in the 1870s. It wasn't until American inventor Leo Baekeland created "Bakelite," an entirely synthetic plastic that did not use cellulose or rubber, that the plastic industry really exploded. Bakelite is made from petroleum products, substances derived from the long-compressed remains of plants and animals found under the earth's surface. Coal, oil, and natural gas are all petroleum products, some of which have been in use for millennia as fuel for fires and for other purposes. The evolution of the modern petroleum industry defined the Industrial Revolution in the Western world, and it is the primary cause of Earth's major pollution problems.

To create Bakelite, Baekeland used phenol, an acid derived from coal tar, inextricably linking plastics to the rapidly growing petroleum harvesting industry. Bakelite was followed by a host of other synthetic plastic polymers, including polystyrene, which was introduced in 1929; polyester, which made its debut just as the Great Depression was hitting in 1930; and polyvinylchloride (PVC), which came about just a few years later in 1933. From the 1930s to the 1960s, plastics were at the height of fashion. Plastic clothing, furniture, cooking utensils, and packaging was eagerly embraced by a society that saw plastics as an innovation and was blissfully unaware of its dark side.

One of the primary problems with plastic is also one of the things that make it so popular; it does not degrade easily. While this means that plastic stands up in even destructive environmental conditions, it also means that plastic waste simply continues to accumulate. This makes plastic very different from the wood and stone that were traditionally used to manufacture household products, which degrade under the influence of the sun, water, weather, and animal and plant infiltration. Plastic, on the other hand, just stays around, for hundreds if not thousands of years. It took a long time for humanity to realize that plastic waste was becoming a major pollution issue, and nearly a century later there is still no answer to this problem. Landfills around the world are brimming with plastic waste, with thousands of tons added each year. In many nations, coping with the buildup of solid waste is a major economic and health issue. The United States currently spends billions of dollars each year to have other countries, largely with developing economies, take and dispose of American waste. This unfortunate industry means that America's plastic waste has become a global problem, with poor, developing nations now struggling to find space to safely dispose of it China was forced to ban the import of plastic waste in 2018, and in 2019 Malaysia announced that it would be forced to ship 3,300 tons of plastic trash back to the United States and Canada.

Plastics will eventually degrade under the influence of heat, light, and water, but even when this finally occurs, it only results in the beginning of a bigger problem. Plastics eventually break up to create what are now called "microplastics," small shards of plastic that then infiltrate smaller and smaller crevices of the environment. Researchers realized how extensive the microplastic problem really was in the twenty-first century. Studies have since shown that the oceans of the world are filled with tons of microplastics, which are responsible for the death of countless marine organisms and the overall degradation of marine environments. In the 2010s, scientists brought a new plastics threat to the attention of Americans, microplastic rain. A 2020 study of eleven remote national park locations around the United States found that microplastics are not only in the water system, but have become part of the water cycle as well. Tiny plastic particles can be carried into the air, mingling in the clouds, until precipitation carries them back to the earth's surface. Researchers found that more than 1000 metric tons of microplastic rains down on US parks and wilderness areas every year. In the Grand Canyon, researchers found that the equivalent of more than 300 million plastic water bottles were essentially being unintentionally littered across the landscape. The discovery of plastic rain is only the tip of a very deep iceberg. Prior to this, the most shocking revelation was the detection of vast areas, larger than many countries, in the Pacific Ocean filled with floating plastic waste and microplastics. Whether on land, sea, or through the air, plastic has become the world's leading pollution problem.

In addition to plastics, thousands of tons of other waste spreads through the water and across the land each year. Industrial processes, including the manufacture of plastic, create toxic chemicals that infiltrate the soil and water supplies, poisoning humans and animals alike. Increasingly, research has shown that many common human illnesses can be traced directly to the products of humanity's industrial growth. From asthma to heart disease, humanity is literally killing itself with its own waste.

Greed and Consequences

Reliance on pollution-heavy petroleum, coal, and natural gas extraction is the primary culprit contributing to environmental degradation. Petroleum harvesting and utilization is pollution-heavy and extremely destructive from start to finish. Mining, fracking, and other techniques produce huge amounts of pollution and necessitate vast destruction of the natural environment. Following this, crude oil is "refined" through a series of processes that also produce liquid and gaseous waste. Finally, petroleum products are burned in the combustion engines used in cars, motorbikes, airplanes, and other vehicles. More petroleum products are burned to heat homes and businesses. The burning of petroleum distributes millions of pounds of gaseous pollution into the skies. These gases rise into the atmosphere where they mingle with other gases, creating poison rain that spills chemicals across the landscape.

It has been widely known since the late 1800s that petroleum excavation and processing was a leading cause of pollution and there has been substantial effort put forth to discover alternative energy sources. However, the effort invested to achieve this goal pales in comparison to that expended to maintain the petroleum industry's growth. Every step forward toward sustainability is a fight against those who personally or professional profit from companies linked to the petroleum industry. These include companies involved in the production of coal and gas directly, but also companies that profit from machines that utilize oil and gas products, such as automobiles, airplanes, household machines like lawnmowers, etc. The companies fighting sustainability also include plastics manufacturers and companies that utilize plastics in their businesses. Fast food restaurants, for instance, fight against efforts to limit single-use plastics. In 2020, Donald Trump received more direct contributions to his political career from oil and gas companies than any other American politician. Official donations receipts indicate that, in that year alone, he received more than $800,000 in donations from these companies. Oil and gas companies have supported Trump's career from the beginning, and have funded many of his political rallies and other initiatives. Further, Trump has personally invested millions of his own inherited estate in oil and gas companies, owning stock in Phillips 66 and other oil companies and in the companies involved in creating the controversial Dakota Access Pipeline, which he has promoted. Trump is not the only politician whose personal wealth and professional careers are dependent on the oil industry, and oil industry executives utilize this leverage to prevent legislation that would force petroleum companies, and related companies, to adopt more sustainable methods. In addition to controlling political action, petroleum companies and allied companies often resort to more insidious methods.

An interesting incident in the 1970s demonstrates the lengths that companies will go to to avoid being held accountable for sustainability. In 1971, an organization named Keep America Beautiful began airing an advertisement featuring a white man dressed as a Native American who sheds a tear when a passing vehicle discards a bag of trash, saying, "Some people have a deep, abiding respect for the natural beauty that was once this country. And some people don't." But the Keep America Beautiful organization was created by plastics manufacturers and petroleum companies and, the goal was to fool Americans into believing that environmental degradation was a public issue, not a corporate one, shifting blame away from themselves. At a time when politicians were considering laws that would have forced beverage companies to stop using plastic, a significant increase in cost, the environmental movement was sufficiently distracted and companies were able to avoid the adoption of these new laws.

Reducing or eliminating pollution is not a goal that can be easily achieved. Though there are many innovative strategies and technologies on the horizon that might help to combat pollution problems, there is no way to fix the problem without adopting serious changes to the use of natural resources. Alternative materials and energies must be explored to replace the petroleum industry. Greta Thunberg, a seventeen-year-old Swedish environmental activist, in 2019, delivered a scathing rebuke at the United Nations in which she lambasted the international community for failing to meet environmental goals, signaling the beginning of a new period of environmental activism.

Works Used

Dunaway, Finis. "The 'Crying Indian' Ad That Fooled the Environmental Movement." *Chicago Tribune.* Nov. 21, 2017. https://www.chicagotribune.com/opinion/commentary/ct-perspec-indian-crying-environment-ads-pollution-1123-20171113-story.html.

"Environmental Impact of the Petroleum Industry." *EPA.* Environmental Protection

Agency. June 2003. https://cfpub.epa.gov/ncer_abstracts/index.cfm/fuseaction/display.files/fileID/14522.

Freinkel, Susan. "A Brief History of Plastic's Conquest of the World." *Scientific American.* May 29, 2011. https://www.scientificamerican.com/article/a-brief-history-of-plastic-world-conquest/.

"History of Plastic." *Dartmouth University.* http://www.dartmouth.edu/~iispacs/Education/EARS18/Plastic_2013/History%20of%20Plastics/History%20of%20Plastics.html.

Knight, Laurence. "A Brief History of Plastics, Natural and Synthetic." *BBC.* May 17, 2014. https://www.bbc.com/news/magazine-27442625.

"Oil and Gas." *Open Secrets.* 2020. https://www.opensecrets.org/industries./recips.php?ind=E01++.

Smith-Schoenwalder, Cecelia. "Malaysia to Ship Plastic Trash Back to the U.S., Other Origin Countries." *USA Today.* May 28, 2019. https://www.usnews.com/news/world-report/articles/2019-05-28/malaysia-to-ship-plastic-trash-back-to-the-us-other-origin-countries.

Wang, Jennifer, "Trump's Stock Portfolio: Big Oil, Big Banks and More Foreign Connections." *Forbes.* Nov. 29, 2016. https://www.forbes.com/sites/jennifer-wang/2016/11/29/trumps-stock-portfolio-big-oil-big-banks-and-more-foreign-connections/#63d3180f464e.

Yurk, Valerie. "Revealed: More Than 1,000 Metric Tons of Microplastics Rain Down on US Parks and Wilderness." *The Guardian.* June 11, 2020. https://www.the-guardian.com/environment/2020/jun/11/microplastics-us-national-parks-survey.

Notes

1. "History of Plastic," *Dartmouth University.*
2. Freinkel, "A Brief History of Plastic's Conquest of the World."
3. Knight, "A Brief History of Plastics, Natural and Synthetic."
4. Smith-Schoenwalder, "Malaysia to Ship Plastic Trash Back to the U.S., Other Origin Countries."
5. Yurk, "Revealed: More Than 1,000 Metric Tons of Microplastics Rain Down on US Parks and Wilderness."
6. "Environmental Impact of the Petroleum Industry," EPA.
7. "Oil and Gas," *Open Secrets.*
8. Wang, "Trump's Stock Portfolio: Big Oil, Big Banks and More Foreign Connections."
9. Dunaway, "The 'Crying Indian' Ad That Fooled the Environmental Movement."

1

Water Pollution

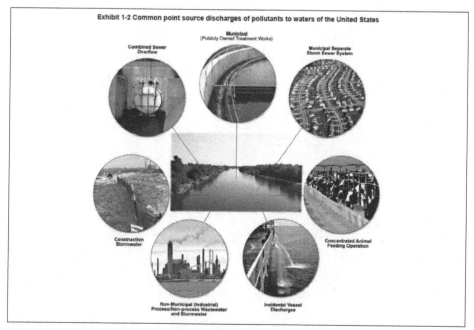

By U.S. Environmental Protection Agency, via Wikimedia.

Common sources of water pollution.

The Stuff of Life

Scientists believe that all life evolved in the world's oceans. For millions of years, the only living things on planet Earth were oceanic organisms, which evolved from simple multicellular creatures into multicellular animals. During this time, nothing lived on the Earth's dry land except bacteria and other single-celled and simple multicellular creatures. It wasn't until around 530 million years before the present that the first animals began to explore the peripheral shores around the ocean. These early pioneers were still tied to the oceanic environment, likely only travelling to other pools or shallows. It was perhaps another 100 million years before plants began to colonize the land, creating new habitats that allowed semiaquatic organisms to explore further from the shores. Prehistoric fish began coming out of the water around 30 million years after plants first appeared on land, beginning a long history of terrestrial evolution that led to humanity in sub-Saharan Africa.[1]

It is often stated that life "left the oceans," but a more accurate representation is that life never really left the water at all. All life on Earth is still dependent on water for survival. The body of the average adult human is around 57 to 60 percent water[2] and, what's more, the bodies of most terrestrial animals are filled not only with water, but with saltwater. The human body is about 0.4 percent sodium chloride (table salt), which is a concentration very much similar to the concentration of salt found in the ocean.[3] Inside the body, there are many microorganisms that need both salt and water to survive and that play different roles in human biology. In other words, the human body is essentially a complex machine filled with a little bit of the ocean. In many ways, terrestrial animals might be comparable to deep sea divers who use pressurized, air-filled suits to explore the ocean. Multicellular organism bodies likewise carry pressurized marine environments over the land.

Living outside of the water also means that multicellular creatures need access to water. Most humans could survive only a couple of days to a week without some form of water, and a significant amount of energy has been devoted to ensuring that water is available for human consumption. This began in prehistory, as ancient human societies learned to divert, redirect, or otherwise carry water from natural sources like lakes, rivers, or underground sources. In the modern world, water from rain and natural sources is channeled through complicated pathways to industrialized facilities that process and "clean" water for human use. The process is incredibly wasteful, such that the average human goes through 80–100 gallons of water each day, which is greater than the amount needed for basic hygiene and survival. All of the water that is diverted for human use is polluted, with both biological and industrial waste, and this waste is then returned to the rivers and streams and eventually ends up in the ocean. The chemical waste from biological and industrial sources is only one part of the pollution that ends up in the Earth's waterways.

There is also large-scale waste, composed largely of discarded plastics and other trash, that ends up in lakes, ponds, rivers, streams, and the ocean. Scientists estimate that humans are responsible for adding 14 billion pounds of trash to the oceans each year. The phenomenon of "plastic pollution" has become one of the leading environmental issues of the twenty-first century, especially after scientists discovered massive areas of polluted marine environments containing plastic waste larger than the country of France. Further research has shown, in fact, that vast portions of the world's oceans are polluted with "microplastics," tiny pieces of plastic debris that have accumulated in the oceans.

Trash and chemical pollution put into the world's fresh and saltwater environments is toxic to life. Each year, millions of animals and plants are destroyed because of water pollution and water toxicity spreads illness, disease, and death. Because all life is dependent on water, all life is ultimately impacted by the build-up of toxic chemicals and other pollutants. Humans ingest dangerous chemicals frequently because those chemicals have infiltrated aquatic environments. Fish and sea creatures whose tissues have been permeated by toxins are ingested around the world and safe drinking water has become more difficult to obtain.

While water pollution sometimes occurs as the result of naturally occurring climatic and chemical processes, the vast majority of pollution is created by humans. Nonhuman animals suffer the most from human-generated pollution because they are dependent on access to water from natural sources, which are frequently heavily polluted. Humans are better able to protect themselves by processing food and water. Pollution may insidiously spread into water supplies or food before scientists and public officials realize it, and scientists have linked many common health issues to pollution unwittingly spread through contaminated food and water. For instance, chemical pollution released into terrestrial environments, even many miles from any water source, may still have an impact on water pollution as chemicals seep through the soil and infiltrate underground water systems.

Ultimately, water pollution threatens all life on Earth. No technology exists that can allow life to survive without access to both freshwater and to the biological nutrients that ultimately come from the oceans before spreading through the earth's ecosystems. If the oceans ecosystems collapse, humanity will go extinct.

Water and History

Anthropologists studying early human history have discovered that the pollution of terrestrial and aquatic habitats began in prehistory with the spread of mass agriculture. In the ancient past, human societies existed by foraging for food and societies tended to be nomadic Anthropologists have found evidence to suggest that, around 12,000 years ago, hunter-gatherers first began experimenting with agriculture. Recent data suggests that there was no single origin point for agriculture, but that it developed simultaneously among several societies living in the Fertile Crescent, a region of what is today called the Middle East. By the time agriculture developed, humans were already cultivating animals, which they carried with them on their nomadic treks.[4] Animal husbandry and agriculture were the keys to allowing humans to create settlements. As these settlements grew into towns, cities, and empires, more food and water was needed, requiring more land. Anthropologists have found evidence to suggest that the pre-Columbian cultures in North America polluted the rivers and lakes they used with agricultural waste, which is still distinguishable as deposits of chemicals and minerals.

Industrialization caused the next massive spike in pollution. Industrialized processes produce more and different kinds of pollution than agricultural activity. The increasing use of often toxic chemicals became the next threat to the integrity of Earth's water reserves. In the beginning, there were no restrictions on industrial activities. Manufacturing facilities freely used lakes, rivers, and the ocean as a dumping ground for toxic chemicals and solid waste. There were local efforts to address this problem, and some American states and cities passed regulations on industrial dumping. In many cases, local laws followed law suits stemming from waste-borne illness or death.

Ohio's portion of the Cuyahoga River has long served as a symbol of water pollution in America thanks to a widely publicized incident in 1969 in which oil and debris floating in the river caught fire. The incident has been called a turning point in American consciousness about water pollution, and the story serves as a microcosm for the history of American water pollution. Like many other major rivers and streams in America, the Cuyahoga River was a primary reason for the founding of the settlement that became the city of Cleveland, Ohio. Access to the river provided food and water, as well as an artery for transportation. Cleveland was a minor city until the Civil War made Ohio a hotspot for industrial manufacturing. At this time, the Cuyahoga River was already used to dump solid and liquid waste from the city and pollution was already threatening both human and nonhuman life, a process that intensified during the Civil War. American Ship Building, Sherwin-Williams Paint Company, Republic Steel, and Standard Oil were all founded in Cleveland and all used the Cuyahoga River to dispose of their chemical and physical waste.

There was so much pollution in the river that the top layer of water caught fire in 1868, 1887, 1912, 1922, 1936, 1941, 1948, 1952, and 1969. Some of these fires were fatal and damaged property, but none resulted in serious changes. The city failed to make improvements or to pass pollution laws even after testing in the 1920s revealed that the toxic water had infiltrated the city's drinking water system, resulting in foul-tasting water linked to health issues. The pollution of the river was in the minds of many people a necessary result of the city's industrial success. It was only when the manufacturing industry in Cleveland began to collapse that citizens became seriously concerned about how the city's industrial era had impacted their home. The Cuyahoga River fire of 1969 was not the worst in the city's history, but it gained nationwide attention at a time when Americans were finally beginning to come to grips with their damaged environment.[5]

The federal government made no national attempt to address water pollution until the Federal Water Pollution Control Act of 1948, which provided the federal government with limited capabilities to force companies to control pollution. During the Richard Nixon administration, in 1972, a series of amendments strengthened federal guidelines on water pollution in the form of the Clean Water Act. The 1972 amendments gave the Environmental Protection Agency (EPA) authority to set standards for processing and disposing of wastewater and provided new regulations on industrial pollution. Federal funding also provided for the construction of new sewage treatment plants to reduce common illnesses transmitted through drinking water.[6]

A Continuing Problem

The establishment of the Clean Water Act was not a solution to water pollution, though it did expand awareness of environmental issues. The framework of the Clean Water Act and similar laws passed at the state and local levels is dependent on the priorities of elected administrators at the municipal, state, regional, and national level. The Donald Trump administration has greatly eroded environmental regulations on clean water, allowing corporations to pollute at a higher level and reducing the capability of the EPA and other regulatory bodies to combat this practice. Trump and members of his inner circle have prioritized industrial profit over public welfare and environmental protection, reflecting the push and pull that dominates American progress on the environment. Corporations that produce pollution typically need to spend more money to meet environmental regulations, so corporate managers and owners spend money to lobby against environmental regulations. Part of this effort involves donating money to candidates for local and federal office. The Republican Party of the twenty-first century has established a reputation as a "pro-business" party and has adopted a platform that prioritizes corporate gain over environmental concerns. Trump has taken this a step further by eliminating EPA regulations on clean water, air, and on other kinds of industrial pollution. This has enabled him to maintain ties and to collect campaign support from leaders in certain industries, and also personally benefits Trump's investment in fossil fuel companies, which are the leading producers of pollution. Prioritization of profit over environmental protection reflects short-term goals, while environmental protection reflects an interest in long-term sustainability and collective benefit.

Works Used

Boissoneault, Lorraine. "The Cuyahoga River Caught Fire at Least a Dozen Times, but No One Cared Until 1969." *Smithsonian Magazine*. June 19, 2019. https://www.smithsonianmag.com/history/cuyahoga-river-caught-fire-least-dozen-times-no-one-cared-until-1969-180972444/.

Chatterjee, Rhitu. "Where Did Agriculture Begin? Oh Boy, It's Complicated." *NPR*. July 15, 2016. https://www.npr.org/sections/thesalt/2016/07/15/485722228/where-did-agriculture-begin-oh-boy-its-complicated.

Fisher, Len. "How Much Salt Is in a Human Body?" *Science Focus*. https://www.sciencefocus.com/the-human-body/how-much-salt-is-in-a-human-body/.

Helmenstine, Anne Marie. "How Much of Your Body Is Water?" *Thought Co*. Feb. 11, 2020. https://www.thoughtco.com/how-much-of-your-body-is-water-609406.

"History of the Clean Water Act," *EPA*. 2020. https://www.epa.gov/laws-regulations/history-clean-water-act.

Wilcox, Christie. "Evolution: Out of the Sea." *Scientific American*. July 28, 2012. https://blogs.scientificamerican.com/science-sushi/evolution-out-of-the-sea/.

Notes

1. Wilcox, "Evolution: Out of the Sea."
2. Helmenstine, "How Much of Your Body Is Water?"
3. Fisher, "How Much Salt Is in a Human Body?"
4. Chatterjee, "Where Did Agriculture Begin? Oh Boy, It's Complicated."
5. Boissoneault, "The Cuyahoga River Caught Fire at Least a Dozen Times, but No One Cared Until 1969."
6. "History of the Clean Water Act," *EPA*.

Lethal Algae Blooms—An Ecosystem Out of Balance

By Jeremy Hance
The Guardian, January 4, 2020

On 3 August 2014, residents of Toledo, Ohio, woke to the news that overnight their water supply had become toxic. They were advised not only to avoid drinking the water, but also touching it—no showers, no baths, not even hand-washing.

Boiling the water would only increase its toxicity while drinking it could cause "abnormal liver function, diarrhoea, vomiting, nausea, numbness or dizziness", read a statement from the City of Toledo, warning residents to "seek medical attention if you feel you have been exposed".

Toledo sits on the shores of Lake Erie, one of North America's five great lakes. About half a million residents of the city and surrounding area have relied on Lake Erie for water for hundreds of years.

After the news broke on 3 August bottled water quickly vanished in concentric circles around the city. Eventually, a state of emergency was called and the national guard arrived with drinking water.

Toledo's water crisis lasted for nearly three days. But the water wasn't toxic due to an oil spill or high lead levels, as in Flint, Michigan. Toledo's water was tainted by something altogether different: an algae bloom.

Toledo is not alone. According to scientists, algae blooms are becoming more frequent and more toxic worldwide.

A 14-month long algae bloom in Florida, known as the "red tide," only ended earlier this year, after killing more than 100 manatees, 127 dolphins and 589 sea turtles. Hundreds of tonnes of dead fish also washed ashore.

In 2018, there were more than 300 reported incidents of toxic or harmful algae blooms around the world. This year about 130 have been listed on an international database, but that number is expected to increase.

Recent reports of a new "red tide" emerging in Florida and more dead wildlife have put the tourist and fishing industries on alert, braced for further devastation.

The causes of the blooms vary, and in some cases are never known, but in many parts of the world they are being increasingly linked to climate change and industrialised agriculture.

What Is Harmful Algae Bloom?

Algae includes everything from micro-algae, like microscopic diatoms, to very large algae, such as seaweed and kelp. Algae are not officially a taxonomic group of creatures (they don't fit into general groups like plants, animals or fungi), but the name is generally used to describe marine or freshwater species that depend on photosynthesis.

An algae bloom occurs when a single member of these species—because of certain conditions—suddenly becomes dominant for a time.

Algae are vital to our survival. It's estimated that at least half of the planet's oxygen comes from these unsung creatures, who produce it through photosynthesis before releasing it into the water. Algae, like land plants, also sequester carbon dioxide; scientists have explored their potential to draw carbon dioxide out of the atmosphere. They have been used as fertiliser, food sources (such as seaweed), and could be a promising source of biofuel in a more sustainable world.

However, some algae blooms can also be harmful—even lethal.

Harmful algae bloom (HAB), as scientists have come to describe the phenomenon, often manifest by forming a kind of scum over a body of water that can be green, blue, brown or even red. But others are completely invisible. The problem has become increasingly widespread and the impact can be deadly to marine life.

Off the eastern coast of the US, a dinoflagellate—a type of marine plankton named *Alexandrium catenella*—has the potential to make shellfish lethal. Its appearance routinely shuts down fisheries, crippling local economies. And it's not just in the US: the same species has shut down mussel farms and recreational collecting of shellfish as far away as New Zealand.

Other blooms wipe out marine life. In 2015, a bloom of various dinoflagellates off the coast of South Africa led to low-oxygen conditions, known as eutrophication, killing 200 tonnes of rock lobster. Freshwater blooms, like those in Lake Erie made up of cyanobacteria or blue-green algae, have not only shut down local water sources but have also been blamed for the death of dogs that had been swimming in them.

It's difficult to make generalisations about harmful algae blooms since specific species have different causes and impacts. Scientists have identified about 100 toxic bloom species in the oceans. Dozens of potentially harmful species of cyanobacteria are known to affect bodies of fresh water.

During most of the past century, harmful algae blooms were rarely headline news, inspiring little scientific study beyond ecological curiosity. That has changed. Algae blooms are notoriously difficult to predict, but a global monitoring group known as HAEDAT is tracking them across the world as they occur. Harmful algae blooms, such as the one that hit Toledo's water supply in 2014, are becoming more common and more toxic—and scientists say humans are to blame.

"There's no question that the HAB problem is a major global issue, and it is growing," said Donald Anderson, director of the US National Office for Harmful Algal Blooms and a lab director at the Woods Hole Oceanographic Institute. "We also have more toxins, more toxic species, more areas and resources affected, and higher economic losses."

Hidden Cost of Ohio's Corn and Soya Bean Boom

The toxic bloom that took over Lake Erie in 2014 was formed by a cyanobacteria known as *Microcystis Aeruginosa,* for which farming is at least partly to blame.

"You have people that still to this day will only use bottled water," says Dr Timothy Davis, an expert in plankton ecology at Bowling Green University, five years after the water crisis and even after Toledo spent $132 million (£101 million) on improving its water treatment plant to handle the blue-green algae.

Lake Erie, the shallowest of North America's Great Lakes, has seen such events in the past. During the 1950s and 60s algae blooms were common, most likely, say researchers, due to poor domestic and industrial wastewater treatment.

"At one point, Lake Erie was considered a dead lake," Davis says. But by the early 1970s, the "dead lake" was resurrected, due to new regulations from the Clean Water Act and the Great Lakes Water Quality Agreement that capped phosphorus loads into the lake at 11,000 tonnes. Phosphorus provides nutrients to plants and is commonly found in manure and produced for fertiliser.

Then in the late-1990s, blooms began to reappear. A cyanobacteria bloom requires two things: nutrients and heat. In the case of Lake Erie, nearby farms have become increasingly reliant on large inputs of synthetic fertiliser.

"We went from agriculture that was small farms [and a] variety of crops to larger commercial farms that were harvested for essentially two row crops, corn and soya beans," says Davis. Today, corn and soya beans are Ohio's top crops.

Employing more fertiliser to feed a global market, the farms' excess phosphorus and nitrogen, another plant nutrient, washed out during storms and into the river and streams that feed Lake Erie. About 80% of the nutrients running into Lake Erie are from sources around the Maumee River, which in this case means agricultural runoff from the surrounding farmland.

"If you have an agricultural system where the farmer can only survive by polluting Lake Erie, then there's something fundamentally wrong with that system," says Dr Thomas Bridgeman, director of the Lake Erie Center.

Since the 1990s, Lake Erie has seen a bloom every year—and they appear to be lasting longer and getting larger. This year's bloom in Lake Erie was the fifth largest since 2002—when monitoring began in earnest. It was 620 square miles at its largest after growing throughout August, before dissipating in September.

Meanwhile, climate change has heated up our planet substantially. Nearby Lake Superior, the most northerly of the Great Lakes and the world's largest, has had its first documented cyanobacteria blooms over the past decade. Before climate change, the lake simply would have been too cold for a long-lasting bloom.

It's now almost a certainty that blooms will continue to appear every summer, say researchers, unless Ohio changes its agricultural practices and the global community finally tackles the climate crisis.

"We have to look around and say, 'Look, what do we grow here?'" says Bridgeman.

"We grow corn and soya beans. Where does the corn go? It goes into our gas tanks. Where do the soya beans go? They go to China, they go to hogs. Is that really what we want to be doing with our watershed?"

> **In 2018, there were more than 300 reported incidents of toxic or harmful algae blooms around the world.**

Algal blooms are also becoming more common and severe in many parts of our oceans, harming wildlife and posing potentially dangerous health impacts for local communities.

Scientists say the "red tide" that stuck around the Florida coast from 2017 through to this year may now be a semi-normal part of the ecosystem.

These blooms are pumping poison into the air, known as brevetoxin, which may be harmful to humans if inhaled. Anyone breathing it in can suffer from uncontrollable coughing and a sore throat. "It doesn't make for a pleasant day at the beach," says Malcolm McFarland, a researcher into algae blooms with the Harbor Branch Oceanographic Institute in Fort Pierce, Florida.

It may have long-term health implications as well—one study found that brevetoxin attacked the DNA of lungs in rats, but further research is needed to understand the impact on human health.

Scientists are less certain about the causes of these red tide marine blooms, but both nutrient runoff and climate change may play a role. "The red tide seems to initiate and peak in the rainy season when runoff from the land is highest, and nutrient inputs to freshwater and coastal water bodies spike," says McFarland.

Meanwhile, on the other side of the north American continent, a different red tide is attacking a different species: California is seeing more sick sea lions taken in by rescue centres; pups and adults are dying.

Scientists believe they are suffering from eating fish tainted by *Pseudo-nitzschia australis* algae. The highly toxic algae are fatal at high doses, both to sea lions and humans.

Unlike Florida's red tides, those in California appear to be a very recent arrival. Until the turn of the millennium, large-scale toxic blooms were rare off the coast of California. Then something changed.

"From [2000] forward, we had a very significant bloom every single year with ecosystem impacts in California, and that has never stopped. Not only that, it seemed as though things were getting more and more toxic," says Clarissa Anderson, the executive director at Southern California Coastal Ocean Observing System, nothing that in less than 20 years of research, scientists have seen toxin numbers multiply by 200—from 500 to 100,000 nanograms per litre of sea water

Anderson says the current best working theory is that increasing carbon sequestration by the oceans—due to the huge increase in greenhouse gas emissions since the industrial revolution—is behind the sudden regularity of these deadly blooms and an increase in their toxicity. She says the study of these events and their toxins is so new that there may be incidents of illness from eating affected fish or shellfish that are misdiagnosed because these poisons are not on the radar of many health organisations.

The Baltic Dead Zones

Europe has had its own experience of deadly algae blooms that now threaten the future of its fisheries. Last year, the Baltic Sea experienced a bloom so large it could have encompassed Manhattan, and it closed beaches from Finland to Poland.

Finland has been systematically sampling its area of the Baltic since 1979, giving us a clearer idea of the spread and growth of the problem, and what's to blame. In that time, blooms have become larger and longer-lasting, creating dead zones and depleting Baltic fisheries.

Like the example in Lake Erie, the Baltic bloom is caused by an influx of nutrients from agriculture and warming waters.

Scientists are regularly tracking nutrient loads from Finland's rivers into the sea. Data from 2014 in the HELCOM Pollution Load Compilation database, the best currently available, found that more than three-quarters of the nutrient load coming into the Archipelago Sea is from agriculture. The number is surprisingly similar to the proportion coming from industrialised agriculture in Ohio.

The Baltic is a brackish water body, thus supporting blooms typical of both fresh and salt water. But, as in Lake Erie, of real concern are cyanobacteria: several species have been known to produce blooms here.

Below the sea's surface there has been a decline in the more nutritious phytoplankton—and food for fish—and an increase in the potentially toxic species in the more southerly parts of the sea since the early 1980s.

Milder winters and increased rainfall pushing more nutrients into the sea, along with higher surface water temperatures—all due to the climate crisis—are also exacerbating factors, say researchers. Blooms usually begin in July and disappear by August or September. But last year a species particularly resistant to cold remained until November.

"The ice was blue-green because of the cyanobacteria under it," says Sirpa Lehtinen, an expert on plankton for the Marine Research Centre with the Finnish Environmental Institute, who adds that scientists are still trying to work out what this all means for the marine ecosystem, and whether fisheries in the Baltic are in serious long-term peril.

Fixing an Ecosystem Out of Balance

So how can we solve a problem like algae? The answer, says Davis, will be part-regional, part-global solutions. For Lake Erie, it will require agricultural changes—including regulations to reduce the nutrient load—and tackling the climate crisis. But solutions elsewhere may be different, for example, blooms in developing countries might require better wastewater treatment.

The 2014 water crisis in Ohio forced the issue politically which hasn't happened in many other places. Governor Mike DeWine recently announced an initiative called H2Ohio, which is expected to include hundreds of millions of dollars for Lake Erie and other Ohio water bodies over the next 10 years. However, scientists say this is not enough.

"It's going to take a lot more money and a lot more political will than what's happening right now," says Bridgeman.

At the Ohio Department of Agriculture, director Dorothy Pelanda said the department was primarily looking at voluntary programmes based on marketing and education for potential solutions such as cover crops and smarter use of fertiliser. In 2014, Ohio passed new regulations on fertiliser use for farms near the lake: such as not spreading before a storm or on frozen fields.

"We know from science that there is not one solution to every farm … It's about education, it's about being sensitive to what works, what doesn't work," she said. She's hoping to provide increased access for farmers to use high-tech, but often expensive, equipment that can give them a better idea of what parts of their land may need fertiliser and how much.

Pelanda said she's also seen interest in diversifying crops beyond corn and soya beans, to grapes, chestnuts and maple sugar. Asked if voluntary programmes will go far enough, Pelanda says: "That's our challenge. We have to get beyond. We're doing these things … but we're not doing enough of these things. We need to really increase the voluntary adoption of these practices."

Others are more sceptical of voluntary approaches. "We have a long history in this country of a farmer does what he wants on his land. You can choose to take advantage of a programme or something, but you can also choose not to," says Bridgeman, who believes local and federal governments can no longer afford to ignore the climate emergency.

"We need to do something about climate change and we're either going to be paying for it by reducing greenhouse gases or we're going to be paying for it by additional treatment of water," says Bridgeman, adding that most of the blooms around the world have a human element to them.

One thing is certain. Algae blooms aren't going away but are yet another sign—like ocean acidification, vanishing Arctic sea ice, and mass extinction of the Anthropocene—"of an ecosystem that is out of balance," says McFarland.

This article was amended on 8 January 2020 to remove a reference to "toxic cryptophytes. Cryptophytes are not toxic. Also, the text was changed to clarify that Baltic bloom in Lake Erie is caused by a range of nutrients, not just nitrogen from farming.

Print Citations

CMS: Hance, Jeremy. "Lethal Algae Blooms—An Ecosystem Out of Balance." In *The Reference Shelf: Pollution,* edited by Micah L. Issitt, 9-14. Amenia, NY: Grey House Publishing, 2020.

MLA: Hance, Jeremy. "Lethal Algae Blooms—An Ecosystem Out of Balance." *The Reference Shelf: Pollution,* edited by Micah L. Issitt, Grey Housing Publishing, 2020, pp. 9-14.

APA: Hance, J. (2020). Lethal algae blooms—An ecosystem out of balance. In Micah L. Issitt (Ed.), *The reference shelf: Pollution* (pp. 9-14). Amenia, NY: Grey Housing Publishing.

Trump Administration Cuts Back Federal Protections for Streams and Wetlands

By Scott Neuman and Colin Dywer
NPR, January 24, 2020

The Environmental Protection Agency is dramatically reducing the amount of U.S. waterways that get federal protection under the Clean Water Act—a move that is welcomed by many farmers, builders and mining companies but is opposed even by the agency's own science advisers.

EPA Administrator Andrew Wheeler, who announced the repeal of an earlier Obama-era water rule in September, chose to make the long-anticipated announcement Thursday in Las Vegas, at the National Association of Home Builders International Builders' Show.

"All states have their own protections for waters within their borders, and many regulate more broadly than the federal government," Wheeler told reporters on a conference call before the announcement.

"Our new rule recognizes this relationship and strikes the proper balance between Washington, D.C., and the states," he added. "And it clearly details which waters are subject to federal control under the Clean Water Act and, importantly, which waters falls solely under the states' jurisdiction."

The biggest change is a controversial move to roll back federal limits on pollution in wetlands and smaller waterways that were introduced less than five years ago by President Barack Obama.

The Obama executive action, which broadened the definition of "waters of the United States," applied to about 60% of U.S. waterways. It aimed to bring clarity to decades of political and legal debate over which waters should qualify.

However, various business interests painted the regulation as a massive federal overreach. Within weeks after the change was announced in May 2015, 27 states sued to block it. At the time, Texas Attorney General Ken Paxton, a leading critic, called the new rule "so broad and open to interpretation that everything from ditches and dry creek beds to gullies to isolated ponds formed after a big rain could be considered a 'water of the United States.' "

The revised rule announced Thursday states that ephemeral bodies of water— those that form only after rainfall or that flow only part of the year and dry up at other times—are among those that are not subject to federal control. This exception also applies to waste treatment systems, groundwater, prior converted cropland and farm watering ponds.

It also identifies four categories that are federally regulated under the Clean Water Act: large navigable waters such as the Mississippi River, tributaries, lakes and ponds, and major wetlands.

"This isn't about what is an important water body. All water is important. This is about what waters Congress intended for the agencies to regulate," Dave Ross, assistant administrator of the EPA's Office of Water, told reporters on the conference call. "And we have clearly established those lines."

However, the revision has also encountered broad criticism. As the proposed rollback was taking shape last year, 14 states sued the EPA over the impending rule change, saying it "ignores science and the law and strips our waters of basic protections under the Clean Water Act."

In a draft letter posted online late last month, the 41-member EPA Science Advisory Board, which is made up largely of Trump administration appointees, said the revised definition rule "decreases protection for our Nation's waters and does not support the objective of restoring and maintaining 'the chemical, physical and biological integrity' of these waters." The letter is signed by the board's chair, Michael Honeycutt.

Gina McCarthy, the EPA administrator under Obama who implemented the 2015 regulation, is among the revision's most vocal critics. Now president and CEO of the nonprofit Natural Resources Defense Council, McCarthy slammed Thursday's announcement.

"So much for the 'crystal clear' water President Trump promised. You don't make America great by polluting our drinking water supplies, making our beaches unfit for swimming, and increasing flood risk," McCarthy said in a statement.

"This effort neglects established science and poses substantial new risks to people's health and the environment. We will do all we can to fight this attack on clean water. We will not let it stand."

In a speech on Sunday at the American Farm Bureau Federation's annual gathering in Austin, Texas, Trump hinted at the change, calling the 2015 Obama rule "one of the most ridiculous regulations of all."

"That was a rule that basically took your property away from you," he said. "As long as I'm president, government will never micromanage America's farmers."

He said the new regulations would "allow states to manage their water resources based on their own needs and what their farmers and ranchers want."

When Trump first proposed the new rule in late 2018, Randy Noel, then chairman of the National Association of Home Builders, told *NPR* that "I'm pretty excited about it because we hadn't had any lots to build on."

Noel lives in south Louisiana, an area with a lot of wetlands. He said developers were running scared because it wasn't ever clear which wetlands were federally regulated and which weren't. "Hopefully, this redefinition will fix that," he said.

But Janette Brimmer, with the legal advocacy group Earthjustice, said in a

> **You don't make America great by polluting our drinking water supplies, making our beaches unfit for swimming, and increasing flood risks.**

statement that under the new rule, "few protections will remain to stop polluters from dumping toxic byproducts into our waters."

The kinds of ephemeral waterways now excluded from federal regulation under the revamped rule make up a large part of the waterways in the arid Southwest and states such as New Mexico.

Rachel Conn, the project director with Amigos Bravos, a New Mexico-based conservation group that focuses on water issues, says those ephemeral streams are important to bigger water systems though, like the Rio Grande.

"And it is from these bigger systems that close to 300,000 New Mexicans receive their drinking water," she says.

Trump ordered a review of the nation's waterways barely a month after taking office. He said at the time that while clean water was "in the national interest," it must be balanced against "promoting economic growth, minimizing regulatory uncertainty, and showing due regard for the roles of the Congress and the States under the Constitution."

Since taking office, Trump has aggressively sought to roll back environmental regulations, particularly those seen as an obstacle to business. According to an analysis by the *New York Times* that was updated a month ago, the administration has revised or eliminated more than 90 environmental rules in the past three years, although several were reinstated following legal challenges and several others are still in the courts.

Print Citations

CMS: Neuman, Scott, and Colin Dwyer. "Trump Administration Cuts Back Federal Protections for Streams and Wetlands." In *The Reference Shelf: Pollution,* edited by Micah L. Issitt, 16-18. Amenia, NY: Grey House Publishing, 2020.

MLA: Neuman, Scott, and Colin Dwyer. "Trump Administration Cuts Back Federal Protections for Streams and Wetlands." *The Reference Shelf: Pollution,* edited by Micah L. Issitt, Grey Housing Publishing, 2020, pp.16-18.

APA: Neuman, S., & Dwyer, C. (2020). Trump administration cuts back federal protections for streams and wetlands. In Micah L. Issitt (Ed.), *The reference shelf: Pollution* (pp. 16-18). Amenia, NY: Grey Housing Publishing.

E.P.A. Is Letting Cities Dump More Raw Sewage into Rivers for Years to Come

By Christopher Flavelle

The New York Times, January 24, 2020

The Environmental Protection Agency has made it easier for cities to keep dumping raw sewage into rivers by letting them delay or otherwise change federally imposed fixes to their sewer systems, according to interviews with local officials, water utilities and their lobbyists.

Cities have long complained about the cost of meeting federal requirements to upgrade aging sewer systems, many of which release untreated waste directly into waterways during heavy rains—a problem that climate change worsens as rainstorms intensify. These complaints have gained new traction with the Trump administration, which has been more willing to renegotiate the agreements that dictate how, and how quickly, cities must overhaul their sewers.

The actions are the latest example of the Trump administration's efforts to roll back nearly 95 environmental rules that it has said are too costly for industry or taxpayers. That list grew on Thursday, when the administration stripped clean-water protections from wetlands, streams and other waterways.

"When you walk into the current E.P.A., as a local government, you're not treated as evil," said Paul Calamita, a lawyer who represents cities seeking to change their agreements. "Which we'd gotten, quite frankly, from prior administrations."

Cities that say they are renegotiating their sewage agreements with the agency include Cleveland; Seattle; Kansas City, Mo.; South Bend, Ind.; and Chattanooga, Tenn. Other cities, including Pittsburgh and St. Louis, have already concluded talks for new terms.

The scale of many of the upgrades required by prior administrations is enormous.

For instance, Washington, D.C., which is considering whether to renegotiate its own deal with the E.P.A., is currently drilling the second of three mammoth tunnels designed for one thing: to hold 190 million gallons of untreated sewage and storm water. The tunnels will be used when the city's aging sewer system is overwhelmed, so that untreated wastewater doesn't flow into the Anacostia River, as it now does 15 to 20 times a year.

While officials in many of these cities praise the Trump administration's flexibility, environmentalists say that the changes threaten safety by allowing pathogens and chemicals to keep flowing into rivers and along beaches and to back up into streets or basements during storms.

"This trend is yet another example of the administration's deregulatory agenda threatening our natural resources and public health," said Becky Hammer, deputy director for federal water policy at the Natural Resources Defense Council. "If cities face genuine cost concerns, there are other methods to maintain affordability while still keeping sewage out of our lakes and rivers."

The latest rollback came on Jan. 23, when the E.P.A. reversed a 2015 rule that protected more than half the nation's wetlands and hundreds of thousands of small waterways. That includes seasonal streams that flow only for part of the year, and wetlands that aren't next to large bodies of water.

Farmers and property developers will now be able to release pesticides, fertilizers and other pollutants directly into many of those waterways, as well as destroy or fill in wetlands for construction projects.

Asked to comment on the E.P.A.'s increased willingness to let cities keep releasing sewage, Michael Abboud, a spokesman for the E.P.A., said in a statement that the agency "has consistently stated that it hopes to achieve full compliance" with the law. "We will continue to work collaboratively with our local partners to ensure that protecting human health and the environment remains the top priority."

Modern federal rules outlaw the release of raw sewage. But older cities across the Northeast and Midwest have older sewer systems designed to carry sewage and rainwater in the same pipes. When rain overwhelms those systems, untreated sewage gets released into local waterways.

Climate change has worsened the problem, causing systems to overflow more often.

Starting in the 1990s, the E.P.A., along with the Department of Justice, began entering agreements that let cities like these avoid fines by committing to detailed plans for reducing or eliminating the overflows. Those agreements, called consent decrees and approved by judges, impose rigid timelines for the work.

Under past administrations, the E.P.A. would sometimes let cities modify these deals, according to Cynthia Giles, who led the agency's Office of Enforcement and Compliance Assurance under President Obama. But the bar was high, she said, citing the example of a major unforeseen disaster that made timely compliance too difficult.

"A consent decree is not the opening bid of a negotiation," said Ms. Giles, who is now a guest fellow at Harvard Law School. "It's a legally binding commitment that is ordered by a federal court."

The tunnel being dug beneath Washington shows the scale of the efforts required to comply with the federal rules.

The city, otherwise reliant on a sewer system that dates as far back as the 1870s, began work a decade ago. Ten stories below Washington, at the end of a two-mile ride on a cramped construction train through a vast tunnel, workers paused recently to explain the mechanics of a 300-foot-long digging machine grinding through the earth.

The digger, a dust-covered tangle of conveyor belts, hoses and thrust cylinders, chews through 60 feet of earth a day. When this section of tunnel is done sometime in 2023, it will be a five-mile-long, 23-foot-diameter tube, built to hold up to 90 million gallons of raw sewage that Washington's increasingly overwhelmed drains would otherwise have to release into the Anacostia River when it rains too hard. It is one of the largest public-works projects in the nation's capital since its subway system was built 50 years ago.

Versions of the tunnel are planned or underway in cities nationwide. Their cost—Washington alone expects to spend $2.7 billion on three tunnels and related infrastructure, funded through higher water bills—has prompted complaints that, among other things, the higher water bills impose a particular burden on low-income people and retirees.

In the Trump administration, the cities have found a sympathetic ear.

In the administration's first three years, the E.P.A. has renegotiated about a dozen consent decrees with cities that use combined-sewage systems, according to Adam Krantz, chief executive of the National Association of Clean Water Agencies, a trade group that represents water utilities. That's almost as many as the 17 that he said the Obama administration renegotiated during eight years in office.

> **The actions are the latest example of the Trump administration's efforts to roll back nearly 95 environmental rules that it has said are too costly for industry or taxpayers.**

Mr. Krantz said he believed about half of the cities with federal agreements for combined-sewage systems were at some stage in the process of renegotiating the agreements. He praised what he called the Trump administration's "more flexible approach toward regulatory and enforcement oversight."

Water utilities "are environmentalists and public stewards," Mr. Krantz said. "To the extent more time or flexibility is requested on a given consent decree, it is because it is needed to attain compliance" with the terms of that agreement.

Mr. Calamita, the lawyer who represents cities seeking to renegotiate, said the administration's position reflected a series of separate policy shifts.

Those shifts include a 2018 directive by Jeff Sessions, who was then attorney general, instructing his department to be what Mr. Calamita described as "more deferential to our local government partners." Then, at the beginning of 2019, Mr. Trump signed legislation directing the E.P.A. to account for the various regulatory requirements a city faces, and the cumulative cost of those requirements.

Mr. Calamita, like others who support the agency's new approach, said cities could not afford the cost of some of the consent-decree requirements, at least not under the timetables they previously agreed to. "They usually cut the best deal the could, figured future E.P.A.s would be more reasonable, and they signed these consent decrees," Mr. Calamita said. "Almost all of my clients have consent decrees they can't afford."

Cities large and small have already renegotiated, including Pittsburgh, which got an extra decade to reduce its overflows; and St. Louis, Mo., which also got an extra five years. Chicopee, Mass., got an extra eight.

Akron, Ohio, has already renegotiated its original 2009 agreement twice, in 2016 and 2019. Officials are now seeking a third amendment, one that would let them avoid building an additional tunnel and other infrastructure that was intended to eliminate overflows completely, according to Ellen Lander Nischt, a spokeswoman for the city.

"It's a very expensive project for very little environmental benefit," Ms. Nischt said, asserting that the amounts of raw sewage that would be released without that tunnel wouldn't cause significant harm.

Mishawaka, Ind., wants permission to scrap a planned storage tunnel. The city, whose current agreement calls for it to stop releasing raw sewage, is also seeking permission for up to nine releases each year, according to Karl Kopec, manager of the municipal wastewater treatment division.

He said the city currently released about 4.2 million gallons of raw sewage annually into the St. Joseph River, down from 300 million gallons in 1990. Eliminating that last 4.2 million gallons would produce "no measurable improvement in water quality in the river," Mr. Kopec said.

Mr. Abboud, the E.P.A. spokesman, said the agency sought to ensure that the terms of the renegotiated consent decree were "at least as protective as the original."

Another city seeking relief is South Bend, Ind., whose mayor until this month was Pete Buttigieg, one of the leading contenders for the Democratic Party's 2020 presidential nomination.

Mark Bode, speaking last month before leaving his post as the city's communications director, said that Mr. Buttigieg had proposed a less-expensive alternative that would reduce overflows by 94 percent. "We expect to come to agreed terms in the coming months," Mr. Bode said.

Washington's utility, DC Water, is considering whether to renegotiate, in the hopes of avoiding the need to build a third storage tunnel, this one along the Potomac River, according to people familiar with the conversations. David Gadis, the chief executive of DC Water, declined through a spokesman to comment.

Tommy Wells, director of Washington's Department of Energy and Environment and chairman of the board of DC Water, said he didn't want the city to reopen that deal. "It's our responsibility to the next generation," Mr. Wells said.

Print Citations

CMS: Flavelle, Chistopher. "E.P.A. Is Letting Cities Dump More Raw Sewage into Rivers for Years to Come." In *The Reference Shelf: Pollution*, edited by Micah L. Issitt, 19-22. Amenia, NY: Grey House Publishing, 2020.

MLA: Flavelle, Chistopher. "E.P.A. Is Letting Cities Dump More Raw Sewage into Rivers for Years to Come." *The Reference Shelf: Pollution*, edited by Micah L. Issitt, Grey Housing Publishing, 2020, pp. 19-22.

APA: Flavelle, C. (2020). E.P.A. is letting cities dump more raw sewage into rivers for years to come. In Micah L. Issitt (Ed.), *The reference shelf: Pollution* (pp. 19-22). Amenia, NY: Grey Housing Publishing.

Great Lakes Waters at Risk from Buried Contaminants and New Threats

By Robert M. L. McKay, Joel E. Gagnon, John Hartig, et al.
The Conversation, December 22, 2019

Nickle Beach, Copper Harbor, Silver Bay. These places, all situated on the shores of the Laurentian Great Lakes, evoke the legacy of mining connected with the region.

While mining operations for metal ores and their refining have all but ceased here, there are renewed concerns over the safety of our Great Lakes source waters. One only has to think back to the 2014 water crisis in Flint, Mich. that exposed more than 100,000 people to elevated lead levels or to more recent headlines over lead contamination in water distributed from Canadian taps.

The Great Lakes basin is home to more than 35 million people distributed across two nations and numerous First Nations. They all rely on this resource for potable water, employment, sustenance and recreational opportunities.

Yet, environmental concerns are a recurring theme, compromising beneficial uses of the lakes and connecting rivers and posing a threat to a combined GDP of US$5.8 trillion across the region.

Canadians have come to expect access to safe, clean and reliable drinking water, as well as access to lakes and rivers for recreational use. However, a legacy of natural resource extraction and industrial use, together with new pressures on freshwater ecosystems, challenge the integrity and sustainable use of these resources.

An A Grade, for Now

Clearly, past environmental crises like mercury pollution of Lake St. Clair in the 1970s, the St. Clair River's blob of perchloroethylene (a dry-cleaning solvent) in 1985, the outbreak of gastroenteritis in Walkerton, Ont. in 2000, the contamination of Michigan's Huron River with PFAS (a family of persistent chemicals) in 2017, and the Flint water crisis provide compelling evidence of the need to control contaminants at their source and avoid another tipping point.

Most people who call Ontario home live within the watershed of one of our four Great Lakes: Superior, Huron, Erie and Ontario. Over 80 per cent of Ontarians receive their drinking water from the lakes.

Considering the high dependency within the province on the Great Lakes, we are fortunate that the protection of these source waters is a priority of Ontario's Clean

Water Act (ON). The province, as recently as 2011, received an A grade in Canada's drinking water report card issued by the environmental law non-profit Ecojustice.

> **Metals, including mercury, PCBs, and other persistent organic compounds top the list of concern.**

Ontario's Source Water Protection Plan began in 2004 on the heels of the tragedy in Walkerton. A total of 38 local plans are currently in place, covering 95 per cent of Ontario's population. Each plan identifies and ranks the risk of land-use patterns, such as locations of waste disposal sites, and effluent threats, such as industrial waste and fertilizers, that could lead to microbial, chemical or radiological contamination.

While the province is doing a good job protecting our Great Lakes source waters to ensure the safety of our drinking water, will these programs continue to protect us into the future and can they address vulnerabilities particular to our Great Lakes?

Heightened Threat from Climate Change?

While the remaining industrial activity on the Great Lakes is regulated, the lakes themselves contain reservoirs of legacy contaminants, mostly in their sediments, that are vulnerable to resuspension. Metals, including mercury, PCBs and other persistent organic compounds top the list of concern. Resuspension is becoming more common under climate change with high water levels, declining ice cover and increased frequency and intensity of major storm events.

In fact, the manifestations of climate change in the region may be placing our drinking water systems at risk from a myriad of threats. These concerns include antibiotic-resistant bacteria, threats from emerging chemicals, increases in discharge from combined sewer overflows and enhanced agricultural runoff of fertilizers and manure, which are implicated in the massive harmful algal blooms that have plagued Lake Erie's western basin in recent decades.

While Source Water Protection Plans provide sound tools for managing our watersheds, we must remain vigilant and develop better risk-based tools that consider legacy and emerging chemical threats especially as they relate to changes to high Great Lakes water levels and increasing intensity of storms.

For example, a sediment disturbance triggered by high winds or shipping accidents could be addressed in a manner similar to chemical spills, closing water intakes until the threat has subsided.

Investing in Our Future

And oversight must go beyond source waters: the renewed concerns in Canada over lead contamination of our drinking water have refocused attention on the need to invest in municipal infrastructure to help ensure a safe and secure water supply.

These investments need to consider old threats, such as replacing lead service lines and antiquated plumbing, coupled with new tools to address growing vulnerabilities related to increased storm-induced discharge events, nutrient remobilization and harmful algal blooms being produced under a changing climate.

The adage holds true—an ounce of prevention is worth a pound of cure!

Print Citations

CMS: McKay, Robert M.L., Joel E. Gagnon, John Hartig, et al. "Great Lakes Waters at Risk from Buried Contaminants and New Threats." In *The Reference Shelf: Pollution,* edited by Micah L. Issitt, 23-25. Amenia, NY: Grey House Publishing, 2020.

MLA: McKay, Robert M.L., Joel E. Gagnon, John Hartig, et al. "Great Lakes Waters at Risk from Buried Contaminants and New Threats." *The Reference Shelf: Pollution,* edited by Micah L. Issitt, Grey Housing Publishing, 2020, pp. 23-25.

APA: McKay, R.M.L., Gagnon, J.E., Hartig, J., et al. (2020). Great Lakes waters at risk from buried contaminants and new threats. In Micah L. Issitt (Ed.), *The reference shelf: Pollution* (pp. 23-25). Amenia, NY: Grey Housing Publishing.

The Missing 99%: Why Can't We Find the Vast Majority of Ocean Plastic?

By Stephen Buranyi
The Guardian, December 31, 2019

Every year, 8m tons of plastic enters the ocean. Images of common household waste swirling in vast garbage patches in the open sea, or tangled up with whales and seabirds, have turned plastic pollution into one of the most popular environmental issues in the world.

But for at least a decade, the biggest question among scientists who study marine plastic hasn't been why plastic in the ocean is so abundant, but why it isn't. What scientists can see and measure, in the garbage patches and on beaches, accounts for only a tiny fraction of the total plastic entering the water.

So where is the other 99% of ocean plastic? Unsettling answers have recently begun to emerge.

What we commonly see accumulating at the sea surface is "less than the tip of the iceberg, maybe a half of 1% of the total," says Erik Van Sebille, an oceanographer at Utrecht University in the Netherlands.

"I often joke that being an ocean plastic scientist should be an easy job, because you can always find a bit wherever you look," says Van Sebille. But, he adds, the reality is that our maps of the ocean essentially end at the surface, and solid numbers on how much plastic is in any one location are lacking.

It is becoming apparent that plastic ends up in huge quantities in the deepest parts of the ocean, buried in sediment on the seafloor, and caught like clouds of dust deep in the water column.

Perhaps most frighteningly, says Helge Niemann, a biogeochemist at the Royal Netherlands Institute for Sea Research, it could fragment into such small pieces that it can barely be detected. At this point it becomes, Niemann says, "more like a chemical dissolved in the water than floating in it."

For the past two years, scientists from the nearby Monterey Bay Aquarium Research Institute have been using customised remote-control submersibles to take samples of the near-invisible plastic drifting far below the surface. "Just because you don't see it, doesn't mean it isn't there" says Anela Choy, a professor of oceanography at the University of California San Diego, and the lead researcher on the project. Below what she calls the "skin surface" of the ocean, the submersibles carefully filter seawater and take a snapshot of what's in it.

Her team found that at a depth of 200m, there were nearly 15 bits of plastic in every liter of water, similar to the amount found at the surface of the so-called garbage patches. The remote samplers were still finding plastic at their maximum depth of 1km. But it is just the start of the hunt. "After two to three years of work the honest truth is we have only one set of samples from one portion of the world's entire ocean," she says.

The group's work is among the first to count the exact amount of plastic below the ocean surface, and to show that plastic waste is abundant at lower depths. Scientists have speculated about this for years. Richard Thomson, the oceanologist who first coined the term "microplastic" in 2004 to describe difficult-to-capture bits under 2mm in length, has suggested that large amounts could be found in the deep ocean and seafloor.

And a 2017 paper from Van Sebille's group predicted that, based on the amount of plastic entering the ocean and the potential ways it is known to sink, 196m tons of plastic may have settled from the surface into the deep ocean since 1950.

The next steps are to show where the plastic comes from, and to ascertain how it moves from the surface, where it is relatively easy to both find and track, to the depths.

The conventional view is that it is very hard to track ocean microplastic back to its source. But even very small bits of plastic don't necessarily look the same. By examining how laser light scatters when it hits different bits of plastic, researchers can create a fingerprint. The plastic found in Monterey Bay, for example, didn't resemble the plastics used in local fishing equipment, but was mostly Polyethylene terephthalate (PET), a polymer used in disposable packing, indicating it probably came from land.

How plastic descends to the deep ocean is, for the most part, a mystery. Because of its low density, most commercial plastic floats. It needs help to get below the surface. Plastic can become attached to ocean detritus that sinks, or fragment under the sun or waves, or find its way into something's stomach.

Choy's team identified two kinds of animals, red crabs and translucent, filter-feeding creatures called giant larvaceans, which consume plastic and moving it to deeper water—either by eating it near the surface and expelling it lower down, or in the case of the larvaceans, in a layer of mucous they periodically discard and let sink.

This sort of unwitting animal transit has been observed in many species. A 2011 study examining plastic in fish in the north Pacific Ocean estimated that they ingested around 12,000 tons a year. In a later paper Van Sebille's group noted that if the number held across the entire ocean, 100,000 tons of plastic could be inside animals at any one time.

On a cool, gray June day in London, Alexandra Ter Halle, a researcher with Paul Sabatier University, in France, was on a sailboat just below Tower Bridge taking samples of water from the Thames. It was the crew's first stop on a tour of 10 European estuaries, and the other scientists on board were doing familiar work, counting microplastic particles with microscopes, and characterising the bacteria in the samples.

Ter Halle's samples, though, would have to wait until she was back at her university, where she has specialized equipment for the detection of nanoplastistics—plastics that have broken down to sizes below a thousandth of a millimeter, smaller than a single cell.

Two years ago her group was the first to detect these particles in seawater. Ter Halle employs techniques similar to those used by forensic scientists to detect chemicals at crime scenes: the samples are ignited into a gas, bombarded with electrons, and separated across an electric field to measure their weight and charge. They can't be conventionally seen, only detected.

Nanoplastic research is still in its infancy. But laboratory tests show that unlike microplastics, nanoplastics are small

> **Plastic ends up in huge quantities in the deepest parts of the ocean, buried in sediments on the seafloor, and caught like clouds of dust deep in the water column.**

enough to accumulate within the bloodstreams and cell membranes of a range of organisms, even passing the blood-brain barrier in a test on Japanese medaka fish, and cause various toxic effects, including neurological damage, and reproductive abnormalities.

"This question of where is all the plastic in the sea … For 40 years we sought out plastic we could see. Now we reach the nanoscale, which is very particular, very reactive, and we have to begin again," says Ter Halle.

The huge amounts of plastic on the ocean surface were what originally sparked public and scientific interest in the plastic problem. In this way, they acted like a buoy, pointing the way to something much larger beneath the surface. The deep ocean is, as Choy puts it, "the world's largest habitat." We're just beginning the accounting of how much of our plastic has ended up there.

Print Citations

CMS: Buranyi, Stephen. "The Missing 99%: Why Can't We Find the Vast Majority of Ocean Plastic?" In *The Reference Shelf: Pollution,* edited by Micah L. Issitt, 26-28. Amenia, NY: Grey House Publishing, 2020.

MLA: Buranyi, Stephen. "The Missing 99%: Why Can't We Find the Vast Majority of Ocean Plastic?" *The Reference Shelf: Pollution,* edited by Micah L. Issitt, Grey Housing Publishing, 2020, pp. 26-28.

APA: Buranyi, S. (2020). The missing 99%: Why can't we find the vast majority of ocean plastic? In Micah L. Issitt (Ed.), *The reference shelf: Pollution* (pp. 26-28). Amenia, NY: Grey Housing Publishing.

Plastic Bags Were Finally Being Banned: Then Came the Pandemic

By Jasmin Malik Chua
Vox, May 20, 2020

In a back room at his home in Santa Cruz, California, George Leonard is amassing a stockpile of plastic bags.

Most of the time, he eschews the things. As chief scientist at Ocean Conservancy, an environmental nonprofit based in Washington, DC, Leonard spends his time campaigning against single-use plastics that can clog up waterways, suffocate wildlife, and take centuries to decompose in landfills.

But that was in the Before Times. Since the Covid-19 pandemic upended life across the globe, ravaging economies and bringing entire health care systems to their knees, everyone is being forced to compromise. Retailers are banning consumers from bringing in their own reusable bags, cities and states are rolling back or delaying single-use plastic bans, and municipalities are scaling back recycling operations, with hygiene fears underlying it all.

With plastic production already projected to increase by 40 percent over the next decade, campaigners like Leonard fear the pandemic could unravel hard-fought measures to pare back the 8 million metric tons of plastic that enters our oceans every year.

The signs so far haven't been reassuring: Customers at Target, for instance, are no longer able to bring in their own bags "out of an abundance of caution, and until further notice," a spokesperson told The Goods, using an oft-repeated phrase. The retailer's in-store recycling kiosks are similarly on hiatus. In early March, the coffee juggernaut Starbucks announced that its baristas would no longer accept customer-proffered mugs. Dunkin' (née Donuts) quickly followed suit.

One by one, the coronavirus knocked long-planned measures off course. In April, New York state announced that its plastic bag ban, which was poised to take effect May 15, would be postponed to mid-June at the earliest. Massachusetts, Maine, and Oregon are deferring similar state laws. New Hampshire has required all grocers to "temporarily transition" to single-use paper or plastic bags only. Even San Francisco, one of the first US cities to outlaw disposable plastic bags in 2007, issued an edict at the end of March preventing businesses from "permitting customers to bring their own bags, mugs, or other reusable items from home." Grocers and retailers in the Golden State are no longer required to charge the previously mandatory 10 cents per disposable bag. And if stores want to stop accepting recyclable bottles, they're free to do so.

Many of these actions are necessary to protect the health of front-line workers who continue to check out groceries, collect trash, and sort through mounds of recycling despite the threat of infection.

"I think they're the appropriate thing to do," Leonard says. "But we're also really worried about whether this pushes us back 10 years in terms of the real progress that has been made to reduce plastic consumption and use, particularly in grocery stores."

Polystyrene, a.k.a. Styrofoam, the non-recyclable plastic that was being phased out pre-pandemic, is having a resurgence as manufacturers such as Ineos Styrolution in Germany and Trinseo in the US see "double-digit percentage sales increases" in the food packaging and health care sectors, *Bloomberg Green* reports.

The pandemic could even reshape long-term behavior. In a 17-page draft document currently under review, the US Centers for Disease Control and Prevention recommends that reopening restaurants switch to disposable menus, plates, and utensils, and swap in single-portion condiments. Who knows how long these and other policies will stick?

Environmentalists also claim that the plastics industry is exploiting Covid-19 fears to demonize reusables as potential vectors for the virus, despite scientific evidence that the contagion can survive for days on plastic surfaces, meaning they're not any safer than your cotton NPR tote or stainless steel Yeti tumbler.

In a letter dated March 18 to Health and Human Services Secretary Alex Azar, Tony Radoszewski, CEO of the Plastics Industry Association, asked the department to "speak out against bans on these products as a public safety risk and help stop the rush to ban these products by environmentalists and elected officials that puts consumers and workers at risk."

Indeed, the plastics industry is currently waging a "PR war" through front groups, corporate-funded research, and misrepresented medical studies in an effort to repeal existing and upcoming bans, says John Hocevar, director of Greenpeace's oceans campaign. Cratering oil prices, which makes virgin plastic cheaper to churn out than ever, aren't helping.

"The plastic industry has really treated the Covid-19 emergency as an opportunity and is preying on people's fear to scare them into believing that single-use plastic is the best way to stay safe," Hocevar says. "And so far, there isn't any independent scientific research that supports that."

Unlike disposable plastics, reusable bags and cups, he says, can be easily disinfected by washing with regular soap and hot water or throwing them in the dishwasher. Grocers might consider letting shoppers bag their own groceries or placing checked-out produce back in the cart so shoppers can load them straight into bins or bags in their cars.

For Hocevar, personal protective equipment (like disposable face masks and gloves) and single-use packaging, discarded carelessly and left to flutter around the environment, pose the bigger threat to public health (not to mention generate even more plastic pollution.)

"I also have concerns about the sanitation workers having to handle so much of this single-use plastic, including PPE, but also food and beverage packaging and bags," he says.

Because We're Staying at Home More, We're Generating More Trash

Disposable plastic bags are only the tip of the landfill, though without comprehensive audits it's impossible to suss out with any certainty if plastic consumption in the country is going up, headed down, or canceling itself out as reduced plastic employment by idling businesses makes up for increasing residential use. But we can extrapolate some trends.

With most restaurants shuttered and Americans hunkered down at home amid widespread lockdowns, takeout and food delivery services—which often employ disposable plastic containers—have skyrocketed in popularity. In the first quarter of 2020, the delivery marketplace Grubhub netted $363 million, a 12 percent jump in revenue over the same period last year. Its number of active diners currently hovers at around 23.9 million, a 24 percent increase from the 19.3 million who placed orders in the first quarter of 2019.

> **Unlike disposable plastics, resuable bags and cups can be easily disinfected by washing with regular soap and hot water or throwing then in the dishwasher.**

Amazon, which shipped more than 3 billion packages a year pre-pandemic, saw its revenue spike by 26 percent to $75.5 billion in the first three months of 2020 after it became a lifeline for shelter-at-homers scrambling for essential goods (toilet paper, Clorox wipes, hand sanitizer) and not-so-essential ones (sex toys, apparently). Most of those deliveries will come swaddled in plastic air pillows, shrink wrap, and polybags.

Working and schooling from home has produced other consequences. Americans are now generating up to 30 percent more trash on a regular basis, says David Biderman, executive director and CEO of Solid Waste Association of North America, a Maryland-based trade group of private and public sector professionals. Some communities—between 60 and 80, by Bideman's count—across the country have placed their curbside recycling programs on hold because they're struggling to devote more staffing power to keep up with the increased residential tonnage. Several material-recovery facilities (or MRFs, pronounced "merfs" in industry parlance) have frozen their operations because it wasn't possible to keep workers 6 feet apart along the conveyor belts where recyclables are manually picked through and sorted.

The problem is, Americans weren't all that great at recycling to begin with. (And that was before China put the kibosh on most of our recyclables.) Of the 35.4 million tons of plastic the US generated in 2017, only 8.4 percent was recycled, according to the Environmental Protection Agency. As waste generation shifts from businesses to homes, Ray Hatch, CEO of Quest Resource Management Group, a sustainability management company in Texas, expects that number to tumble even further.

"The businesses we serve are quite disciplined, and they have processes to separate materials, whether it's plastics or cardboard, correctly," Hatch says. "Households are less dependable, frankly, than businesses. There's a lot of contamination, there's misunderstanding about what goes where. We're going to have a whole lot more going into the landfill, I'm afraid."

Eric Goldstein, senior attorney and New York City environment director at the Natural Resources Defense Council, for one, says he's hopeful that these adjustments in behavior, whether on the personal, state, or federal level, are temporary. The environment may be taking a hit now, but what matters more is how we respond in the long run.

"We are in distress conditions now," Goldstein said. "We're in the middle of the war, and so sometimes you've got to jury-rig temporary solutions to address concerns, even if they later proved unfounded. But when you're talking about sustainability, it's long-term trends and the direction of policy that's important."

Environmentalists Say We Need to Keep Our Eye on the Bigger Picture: Climate Change

Before Covid-19 reared its head, consumer opinion about the need to reduce single-use plastic consumption was at an "all-time high" and is unlikely to have changed, says Miriam Gordon, program director at Upstream Solutions, a California environmental nonprofit that helped spearhead Berkeley's Single-Use Foodware and Litter Reduction Ordinance, which does not go into effect until next year.

"People do not have to choose one crisis over another," Gordon says. "The plastic pollution and climate crises are much more long-term threats to our health, wealth, and environmental sustainability than the Covid-19 crisis."

Not only does plastic have a cradle-to-grave impact on climate change, as the *Guardian* reported in 2019, but disposable food-and-beverage packaging is also full of hazardous chemicals that can migrate into the items we consume. More important, we only have a matter of years to pump the brakes on carbon emissions, limit temperature increases to 2 degrees Celsius above preindustrial levels, and avert the worst effects of a climate catastrophe—think oppressive drought, severe storms, calamitous wildfires, and other hallmarks of extreme weather.

There are glimmers of positivity, however.

In 2018, the UK-based Ellen MacArthur Foundation launched the New Plastics Economy Global Commitment, a worldwide initiative of more than 400 businesses—including Apple, Burberry, Coca-Cola, PepsiCo, Starbucks, Target, and H&M—that aims to eliminate all "problematic and unnecessary" plastic items by 2025. But despite the fiscal squeeze from roiled supply chains and reduced consumer spending, the foundation hasn't seen any backtracking from signatories since the pandemic began.

"There might be some delay in progress, but not to the extent that the targets will be changed or targets will be withdrawn," says Sander Defruyt, lead of the New Plastics Economy initiative. "I think they all realize that if we emerge from this crisis, the plastic pollution and waste issue will still be there."

Certainly, for all we harp on individual responsibility, corporate action and government policy are necessary to pull us from the brink of environmental disaster. We're not going to solve climate change by changing light bulbs in our house, Leonard says. Rather, we need a "fundamental rethinking and restructuring of our energy systems."

That's not to say that what we do doesn't matter, though. "Individual choices do send signals; they send signals into the market, and they send signals into the political arena," he adds. "And obviously, elected officials are responding to the collective will of their constituents."

Still, Leonard points out that nobody should feel guilty about their personal choices as they adjust to this new abnormal. He isn't happy about having to use disposable plastic bags at the supermarket either, but he recognizes that they help reassure front-line workers.

"Everybody should kind of do their part to live a sustainable lifestyle, but also recognize that their choices are limited by the larger society and governance structure in which we live," Leonard says. "So we're not big fans of civil disobedience in this regard."

The platitude that we're all in this together may be trite and maudlin, but never has a sentiment been truer. "We need to think collectively about how we get to the other side," he says.

Print Citations

CMS: Chua, Jasmin Malik. "Plastic Bags Were Found Being Banned: Then Came the Pandemic." In *The Reference Shelf: Pollution,* edited by Micah L. Issitt, 29-33. Amenia, NY: Grey House Publishing, 2020.

MLA: Chua, Jasmin Malik. "Plastic Bags Were Found Being Banned: Then Came the Pandemic." *The Reference Shelf: Pollution,* edited by Micah L. Issitt, Grey Housing Publishing, 2020, pp. 29-33.

APA: Chua, J.M. (2020). Plastic bags were found being banned: Then came the pandemic. In Micah L. Issitt (Ed.), *The reference shelf: Pollution* (pp. 29-33). Amenia, NY: Grey Housing Publishing.

2
Clean Air

By NASA Aqua MODIS/Worldview.

Since the 1960s, astronauts have been photographing air pollution from space. Above, haze hovers over the Northeast in 2012, possibly from sun, humid air, and smoke from western wildfires. Although a rare occurrence, haze can sometimes be so concentrated that the landscape below disappears.

Waiting to Inhale

There are five essential gases—nitrogen, oxygen, water vapor, argon, and carbon dioxide (CO_2)—that compose "air," the fluid medium that fills earth's lower atmosphere and is directly responsible for the continuation of life on Earth. There are many other elements that also appear in the air in trace amounts, such as neon or methane.[1] Earth's atmosphere is a byproduct of life on earth, which in turn depends on the composition of the atmosphere remaining within a certain range. If the chemical composition of the atmosphere varies too far from this ideal range, organisms begin to experience physiological dysfunction that can ultimately be fatal.

All organisms require certain elements and compounds. many of which are obtained through respiration, which is the process of taking in gaseous elements from the atmosphere and returning a different composition of gases back to the environment. The current composition of the atmosphere is largely the product of the evolution and spread of plant life. Plants take in carbon dioxide from the environment and use it to produce sugars that fuel cellular activity, growth, and reproduction. Plants then release oxygen into the atmosphere. Plants therefore play a dominant role in determining the composition of the air. For instance, during the Carboniferous Period (roughly 400 million to 290 million years ago), huge forests spread across the world and there were relatively few animals. As a result, massive forests stripped the atmosphere of carbon and filled it with high concentrations of unstable oxygen gas. Humans could not have lived in such an environment, as the concentration of oxygen was too high and the superoxygenated atmosphere was so unstable that a minor electrical shock could set off vast wildfires. During this period the remains of burned plants and animals were buried under sediment, creating the vast coal and oil reserves that humans utilize to create energy.[2]

As animal life evolved and spread across the earth, the composition of the atmosphere changed. Unlike plants, many animals absorb atmospheric oxygen and, through a series of chemical processes, breath out carbon dioxide, nitrogen, and methane into the air. Plants are then able to absorb these gases from the air, and return oxygen to the atmosphere. Plants and animals therefore exist in a balanced respiratory cycle. For humans and other animals to survive, there must be a balance of plant and animal life. If plant life is reduced to too low a level, there will be insufficient oxygen and higher levels of carbon dioxide. If this continues past a certain level, animal life will no longer be able to survive.

Through the use of technology, humanity has a more rapid and dramatic impact on the atmosphere than any other species. Anthropologists aren't certain when humans harnessed the power of fire, but since then humanity has been producing more and more smoke and soot, by-products from burning organic compounds, and these chemicals have entered earth's atmosphere, dramatically altering the composition of air itself. As humans burned wood and other organic materials for heat and later too power machines, the composition of earth's atmosphere has changed for the worse. Forests were also cut down, wetlands and swamps were filled in, and water systems were poisoned with industrial waste. Plant life diminished and, the system that keeps the earth's atmosphere in balance eroded. Modern humans breathe air polluted with massive doses of often toxic chemicals and the buildup of CO_2 and other gases in the atmosphere is raising the temperature of the earth. This is causing sea levels to rise, storms and climatic disturbances to become more frequent and violent, and the deserts of the world to grow at an alarming rate. Air pollution is one of the key factors in the climate change crisis, and, like water pollution, poses an existential threat to human existence.

Recognizing the Problem

Air pollution is often an invisible threat. However, when fossil fuels like coal and oil are burned, toxic gases leave an immediately recognizable mark. Smokestacks from industrial plants around the world spew millions of tons of soot and smoke into the air each day. In the modern world, technology has made it possible to remove some of the harmful pollutants from the gases, but this was not always the case. Concern about air pollution did not surface until the late 1800s, cities shifted toward industrial, manufacturing economies. Several US cities passed their first air pollution legislation, designed to control the emission of "smoke." Concern about air pollution from the 1800s into the late twentieth century tended to be seasonal and was related to what are called "inversions." During the winter, changes in air pressure and density can cause pollutants that are typically present higher in the atmosphere to descend toward the ground. When this occurs, pollution levels can rise dramatically in cities and industrial towns, leading to illness and even death. It was during extreme winter inversions that legislators and activists first began pushing for air pollution solutions.

The first air pollution law known in the Western world was passed in 1306 by King Edward I of England, who placed a ban on burning "sea coal," which created a deadly toxic haze in winter, in the city of London. The next law wasn't passed until 1873, when a dense smog created by coal-burning killed at least 268 Londoners. In 1881, the first municipal air pollution laws appeared in the United States, with cities like Chicago and Cincinnati enacting "smoke abatement" laws that limited the number of hours in which factories, railroads, and ships could release smoke into the air. The term "smog," a combination of the terms "smoke" and "fog," was coined in Glasgow, Scotland, by Dr. Harold Antoine Des Voeux, in a written report about a winter fog in Scotland believed to be responsible for more than 1,000 deaths.

Eventually, better systems for removing smoke from industrial emissions eased concerns about air pollution, and the issue didn't resurge until the mid-twentieth century. In the United States, the Public Health Service (PHS) first began looking into air pollution in the 1920s. A 1928 report from the PHS found that sunlight levels had been reduced by 20 to 50 percent in New York City as a result of pollution. The next major step forward came in St. Louis, Missouri, when a November 1939 inversion led to nine days of extreme pollution that darkened city streets to the point of near-zero visibility, and street lights remained on during the day. It is unknown how many died or became ill due to this incident, but it led to the first strong air pollution legislation in the country as city and business leaders cooperated to switch to a low-quality coal system that produced less pollution. Similar smog incidents in Los Angeles also provoked smoke legislation during the late 1940s. But the most extreme air pollution crisis in the United States came in 1948 in the coal-mining town of Donora, Pennsylvania. That year, unusual climatic conditions created an intense inversion that killed at least 20 people, while at least half of the town's 14,000 residents became ill due to breathing the toxic air. The deadliest smog-related incident came four years later across the Atlantic Ocean, when a fog containing high concentrations of sulfur gases killed an estimated 12,000 London residents.[3]

Congress passed the nation's first federal law on air pollution, the Air Pollution Control Act, in 1955, giving federal authorities the right to force corporations to reduce pollution and also creating funding for new technologies to reduce pollution. England was directly on the heels of the United States, passing the Clean Air Act in 1956, which likewise gave UK governmental agencies the power to force corporations to reduce emissions.[4]

The air pollution regulations of the 1950s failed for a number of reasons. In a pattern repeated throughout American history, politicians and corporate leaders prioritized short-term profit over long term considerations of public health and safety. Profit may be limited by the cost of environmental remediation or simply by the fact that higher production translates into higher levels of pollution, and so controlling pollution can mean limiting productivity. In any case, politicians, many supported directly by lobbyists from heavy-pollution industries like coal mining, oil exploration, lumber, and chemical manufacturing, were unwilling to take a strong stance on pollution and so the federal legislation of the 1950s produced only minor changes. Smog events continued to occur, though none as deadly as those experienced in the late 1940s, thanks to improved technology for managing industrial waste.

A surge in environmental awareness, driven by activists, writers, and researchers who showed Americans how smoke and air pollution was harming forests and animals, led to environmental improvements and the Clean Air Act amendments of 1967. These were further updated just three years later under the Nixon administration, and the amended laws established air quality standards, which are used to measure and report on air pollution hazards that may impact public health. The 1970 revisions further created a new set of standards for new manufacturing facilities and became part of the newly created Environmental Protection Agency's mandate to protect the public and the environment from the damaging impact of corporate activity.

Though pollution emissions have been linked to climate change politicians in many countries responsible for most of the world's air pollution continue to support legislation that benefits companies at the expense of public health. Under the Donald Trump administration, the EPA has been deprived of much of its funding, power, and influence, while the White House has called for a reduction in air pollution regulations. Trump and supporters claim that EPA regulations were unnecessarily onerous, reducing economic growth at an unacceptable rate. Studies have routinely shown that EPA regulations, while reducing profit for fossil fuel companies and other major producers of air pollution, do not hamper economic growth or productivity. Trump, who has personally invested millions in fossil fuel industry companies, profits from reducing EPA regulation. Further, Trump and many allied politicians have received financial support in their careers from pollution-producing corporations.

A Compound Problem

America is in the midst of its most openly antienvironmentalist federal government of the past 50 years, and the debate over environmental issues has intensified. Some have argued that technological changes can be made to limit environmental damage while intensifying the growth of the fossil fuel industry. Though this claim has been widely circulated, there appears to be little substance to this idea. For instance, while the Trump administration touted the benefits of near "clean coal" technology, studies have shown that the technology produces more pollution than traditional coal mining and burning.

Ultimately, the fossil fuel industry is at the root of the world's air pollution problems. A final solution to the problem will require moving away from coal, oil, and all petroleum products and shifting industrial production towards solar, wave, and geothermal sources of energy. Progress in these areas has been steady and considerable, but insufficient to significantly reduce the world's reliance on pollution-heavy sources of energy. In 2020, as the world is experiencing major tumult related to the Covid-19 pandemic and to protests over police brutality, broader environmental issues have taken a back seat to the world's medical and social justice issues. But studies have shown that there is a relationship between air pollution and the Covid-19 pandemic and that areas with higher levels of air pollution saw a higher number of more severe Covid cases. During the widespread municipal and state "lockdown" orders of March, April, and May of 2020, scientists saw air pollution levels falling, in a large part due to reduced automotive traffic, but this pattern was temporary. Within a short period of time, pollution returned to pre-lockdown levels.[5] Any individuals with respiratory difficulties or illness or who are at risk for respiratory problems are at higher risk in areas with higher levels of pollution. Studies also indicate that the Covid-19 disease disproportionately impacted communities of color in the United States, because individuals in these communities have less access to resources and medical care. Poor individuals, and individuals of color, were therefore more exposed to risk from contracting Covid-19 and faced a shortage of resources for those suffering from the disease. Environmental threats also disproportionately impact poor people and people of color because of the same lack of resources that leave these communities at risk from environmental and other social perturbations.

Works Used

"Covid-19 Lockdowns Significantly Impacting Global Air Quality." Science Daily. May 11, 2020. https://www.sciencedaily.com/releases/2020/05/200511124444.htm.

Helmenstine, Anne Marie. "The Chemical Composition of Air." July 7, 2019. https://www.thoughtco.com/chemical-composition-of-air-604288.

"Historical Perspective on Air Pollution Control," in Safe Design and Operation of Process Vents and Emission Control Systems. Center for Chemical Process Safety. New York: John Wiley & Sons, Inc., 2006.

Potenza, Alessandra. "In 1952 London, 12,000 People Died from Smog—Here's Why That

Matters Now." The Verge. Dec. 16, 2017. https://www.theverge.com/2017/12/16/16778604/london-great-smog-1952-death-in-the-air-pollution-book-review-john-reginald-christie.

Zalzal, Kate S. "A Flammable Planet: Fire Finds Its Place in Earth History." Earth. Jan. 16, 2018. https://www.earthmagazine.org/article/flammable-planet-fire-finds-its-place-earth-history.

Notes

1. Helmenstine, "The Chemical Composition of Air."
2. Zalzal, "A Flammable Planet: Fire Finds Its Place in Earth History."
3. Potenza, "In 1952 London, 12,000 People Died from Smog—Here's Why That Matters Now."
4. "Historical Perspective on Air Pollution Control," Center for Chemical Process Safety.
5. "Covid-19 Lockdowns Significantly Impacting Global Air Quality," Science Daily.

What Causes Asthma? Clues from London's Great Smog with Implications for Air Pollution Today

By Jamie T. Mullins
The Conversation, July 26, 2016

Asthma is a chronic respiratory condition with no known cure. It impacts people of all ages through episodic constrictions of the airways, which may be even worse than it sounds. Approximately 334 million people worldwide suffer from asthma, including 24 million Americans and 5.4 million residents of the U.K., and the average annual cost of each case has been estimated to be between $US2,300 and $4,000.

Our understanding of the triggers of acute asthma episodes—often called "asthma attacks"—has developed significantly in recent years, and techniques for managing asthma over the long term have also advanced. Yet the number of people who suffer from asthma continues to grow, and we still don't know what causes the condition to develop in the first place.

In a recent study, my coauthors and I used an unexpected exposure to a major air pollution event—the Great London Smog of 1952—to demonstrate that air pollution exposure in early life leads to higher incidence of asthma during both childhood and adulthood. While London's air is much cleaner today than it was 60 years ago, our findings have major implications for the many countries that continue to struggle with high levels of urban air pollution.

The Great Smog

The Great Smog took place in London over five days in early December 1952. During that time, a layer of warm air settled over the city, trapping colder air near ground level. The cold air drove Londoners to pile coal on their fires to keep warm, and the upper layer of warm air trapped the resulting smoke near the ground where it mixed with a heavy fog.

The smog that resulted was so thick in places that visibility was said to have fallen to 12 inches. Bus, airplane, taxi and other services were halted, and drivers who braved the roads were forced to rely on others to walk ahead of the vehicle, calling out instructions and warning pedestrians. More than 100,000 people were treated for pneumonia or bronchitis, hospital wards filled to overflowing and morticians reported an inadequate supply of coffins in which to store the dead.

Ultimately, some 3,000 to 4,000 "extra" deaths—that is, deaths above the normal rates which are attributed to the abnormal conditions—occurred during the Great Smog. Approximately 8,000 more cardiac and respiratory deaths over the next several months have also been linked to the smog. The toll of the Great Smog was so large that it ultimately served as a major impetus for the passage of the 1956 and 1968 U.K. Clean Air Acts.

The Link to Asthma

Our paper examines long-term impacts of the Great Smog on people who were exposed very early in their lives. To do this, we used data collected as part of the English Longitudinal Study on Aging. First, we compared the increase in asthma rates among the cohort of London-born children exposed at early ages to the Great Smog to the asthma rates among London-born children in other age cohorts. This provides the impact of the Great Smog on the asthma rates of those living within London. We next compared this change in asthma rates to the difference in rates between the same age cohorts of children living outside of London at the time of the Great Smog.

This difference-in-differences approach controls for the higher rates of asthma that are generally prevalent among city-dwellers. It also accounts for any changes in asthma rates that occurred both within and outside the area affected by the Great Smog around the time of the event, such as general trends in asthma rates and diagnoses.

In our analysis, we found that people who were exposed to the Great Smog during the first year of life were four to five times more likely to develop asthma as a child and three times more likely to report asthma as an adult compared to baseline rates. We also found evidence suggesting that children who were exposed to the Great Smog in utero suffered twice the normal rate of childhood asthma. Our results indicate that early exposure to air pollution has significant long-term impacts on health, and contributes to the development of asthma.

> **While there is a strong consensus that exposure to air pollution negatively affects health, our work presents some of the first evidence that such exposure has lifelong consequences.**

Our approach treats the Great Smog as a natural experiment, allowing us to rule out many alternative explanations for observed increases in asthma rates. This framework reduces the range of factors that could be contributing to the increased rates of asthma among those exposed at early ages and allows us to convincingly link exposure to the Great Smog during the first year of life with higher incidences of asthma in both childhood and adulthood.

The Importance of Early Exposures

While air pollution is known to trigger asthma attacks, neither short- nor long-term exposures have previously been linked so clearly to the initial development of the condition. By demonstrating the connection between early air pollution exposure and the later development of asthma, our findings fill an important gap in our understanding of the condition, and provide actionable information for doctors, policymakers and parents.

Our results suggest that reducing exposure to extreme air pollution events, especially among the young, may be an effective means of combating the initial development of asthma. By improving air quality and protecting young children from air pollution, policymakers and doctor/parent teams may be able to meaningfully reduce the likelihood of asthma in individual children and the incidence of asthma in the population as a whole.

Our findings also dramatically illustrate the long-term effects of air pollution exposure. While there is a strong consensus that exposure to air pollution negatively affects health, our work presents some of the first evidence that such exposure has lifelong consequences. The London Smog took place more than 60 years ago, but some of those that lived through it are still feeling its impacts today.

Urban Air Pollution Today

Such long-term effects have ominous implications for the millions of people around the world who are exposed regularly to extreme air pollution. In a recent article, Douglas Dockery and Arden Pope—two of the foremost researchers on air pollution and health—noted that conditions during a 2013 air pollution event in Harbin, China were "remarkably similar to those from London during the 1952 Great Smog."

Unfortunately, such extreme air pollution is both a widespread and growing problem. Beijing suffered some of its worst recorded air pollution at the end of 2015. And for all of the attention that air quality in China has received since the Beijing Olympics, none of its cities even makes the list of the top 20 most polluted in the world. Much of the urban population in emerging Asia, the Middle East and Africa regularly face more extreme levels of air pollution. Our results suggest that the negative health impacts of these exposures will last for many years to come.

Print Citations

CMS: Mullins, Jamie T. "What Causes Asthma? Clues from London's Great Smog with Implications for Air Pollution Today." In *The Reference Shelf: Pollution,* edited by Micah L. Issitt, 43-45. Amenia, NY: Grey House Publishing, 2020.

MLA: Mullins, Jamie T. "What Causes Asthma? Clues from London's Great Smog with Implications for Air Pollution Today." *The Reference Shelf: Pollution,* edited by Micah L. Issitt, Grey Housing Publishing, 2020, pp. 43-45.

APA: Mullins, J. (2020). What causes asthma? Clues from London's great smog with implications for air pollution today. In Micah L. Issitt (Ed.), *The reference shelf: Pollution* (pp. 43-45). Amenia, NY: Grey Housing Publishing.

Air Pollution Could Make the COVID-19 Pandemic Worse for Some People

By Justine Calma
The Verge, March 19, 2020

Juliana Pino usually fights to push polluters out of the Little Village neighborhood of Chicago, an industrial area with a big Latino community. Now, amid the ongoing novel coronavirus pandemic, she and her colleagues are also checking in on their elderly neighbors, pooling money together for groceries to help those who can't afford them, and translating health information on the novel coronavirus for Spanish-speaking residents. The work is different, but it's still connected to her fight for clean air.

The older people who live in Little Village are already more vulnerable to COVID-19 because of their age. But the ones who grew up here also spent most of their lives breathing in air laden with the soot from nearby coal power plants, she explains. "You have a legacy of toxic exposure paired with a lot of social vulnerability, that means that the same pound of pollution impacts different people differently," says Pino, a policy director for the Little Village Environmental Justice Organization, which successfully campaigned to close the coal power plants in 2012.

Inequities Have Real Consequences and COVID-19 Will Show That

The novel coronavirus is changing nearly every aspect of life in places with an outbreak. Like any disaster, the COVID-19 pandemic will hit some people harder than others. Since it's a disease that affects the lungs, people who live in places with way more air pollution could be more vulnerable. This pollution tends to be worse in communities with more poverty, people of color, and immigrants.

When it comes to the US, "We're the richest country in the world yet we have some of the greatest inequities. These inequities have real consequences and COVID-19 will show that," John Balmes, a physician and a spokesperson for the American Lung Association, tells The Verge. "The air pollution interacts with multiple other factors that increase risk," he says.

Severe cases of COVID-19 can lead to pneumonia, which can kill. The disease is deadliest in older people and those with preexisting health conditions that make it harder to breathe or fight off the infection. Even without a pandemic, living with air pollution has been linked to higher rates of lung disease like asthma and chronic obstructive pulmonary disease (COPD) in populations. High levels of air pollution have also been linked to larger numbers of people hospitalized with pneumonia, studies in the US and China have found.

Air pollution was already a problem in the area and so was making ends meet. That's a double whammy of higher risk and fewer resources.

During the 2003 SARS outbreaks, which was caused by another coronavirus, patients from places with the highest levels of air pollution were twice as likely to die from SARS compared to those who lived in places with little pollution, a study on SARS cases in China found. Even moderately bad air pollution significantly increased the risk of death.

There isn't data yet on how air pollution is playing into the current pandemic, but Balmes points out that international hotspots for COVID-19—Wuhan, Northern Italy, and South Korea—have pretty high levels of air pollution. He believes air pollution may be one reason, although not the primary factor, for why outbreaks in those places have been so devastating.

Another data point from China backs up the air pollution hypothesis. More men have died from the novel coronavirus in China than women, and there's been some speculation that this could be because fewer women there smoke. If smoking does put someone at higher risk, then the same is probably true of air pollution, Ana Navas-Acien, a physician-epidemiologist at Columbia University, tells The Verge. "If we extrapolate from there, we could speculate that maybe individuals, communities that have higher air pollution levels could also be at higher risk of developing a more severe infection," she says. "It's a hypothesis at least worth testing."

In places like Chicago's Little Village neighborhood, the COVID-19 pandemic is piling on top of other stressors. Social distancing immediately took its toll on the city's street vendors, a majority of whom live in the neighborhood, according to Pino. "It's like today, right now, they can't afford the groceries because they would have taken that day's cash to go get supplies," says Pino. "It's those folks in really precarious day-to-day situations that the community's rallying around—even still, it's not enough," she says.

Higher Risks and Fewer Resources

Air pollution was already a problem in the area and so was making ends meet. That's a double whammy of higher risk and fewer resources. "Researchers call this the double jeopardy hypothesis and it can be extended to something like the novel coronavirus pandemic we are now facing," Anjum Hajat, an epidemiologist at the University of Washington, said in an email to The Verge. That "double jeopardy" is often used to describe disadvantages that elderly people of color face because of both their age and race.

Balmes also worries about how poor housing and not enough green space or healthy foods in polluted neighborhoods increase risks. Some immigrants may have an even harder time getting care because of the fear of deportation, he fears.

Fewer cars on the road and planes in the air have temporarily curbed pollution in China, Italy, and California. But it doesn't erase the decades' worth of damage that's been done. That's why, Pino says, "we need to see targeted, prioritized help to the communities that are being hit hard now."

Print Citations

CMS: Calma, Justine. "Air Pollution Could Make the COVID-19 Pandemic Worse for Some People." In *The Reference Shelf: Pollution*, edited by Micah L. Issitt, 46-48. Amenia, NY: Grey House Publishing, 2020.

MLA: Calma, Justine. "Air Pollution Could Make the COVID-19 Pandemic Worse for Some People." *The Reference Shelf: Pollution*, edited by Micah L. Issitt, Grey Housing Publishing, 2020, pp. 46-48.

APA: Calma, J. (2020). Air pollution could make the COVID-19 pandemic worse for some people. In Micah L. Issitt (Ed.), *The reference shelf: Pollution* (pp. 46-48). Amenia, NY: Grey Housing Publishing.

Black People Are Dying from the Coronavirus—Air Pollution Is One of the Main Culprits

By Jared Dewese
The Hill, May 24, 2020

During the turmoil of the coronavirus pandemic, we're hearing often from our leaders that "we're all in this together." While true, some of us are in it more than others; black Americans are dying at a faster rate from the novel coronavirus than other groups. There are many reasons for this disparity, but a big one that's getting too little notice is one of the many systemic failures endangering black Americans: their exposure to air pollution.

Harvard researchers recently found that even the smallest increase of exposure to a common air pollutant is associated with a 15 percent increase in the death rate from COVID-19 (on top of increased risk of lung cancer and heart problems). Fossil fuel plants are among the top emitters of this particle, along with other pollutants that can cause or worsen asthma and shortness of breath. Partly due to a history of redlining, African Americans live closer to fossil fuel infrastructure than the rest of the population: A 2017 joint report from the National Association for the Advancement of Colored People and the Clean Air Task Force found that more than a million African Americans live within a half-mile of an oil and gas facility.

The impact is clear and stunning. Right outside the gates of the White House, African Americans make up 80 percent of COVID-19 related deaths in Washington, D.C., while we compose less than 50 percent of the population inside the beltway. Seventy-two percent of those who have died from the virus in Chicago have been black, despite making up only about 29 percent of the city's population. In Michigan, 40 percent of those dead from COVID-19 were black, but only 12 percent of the state is black.

The story is just as staggering in Louisiana, where parts of the 85-mile stretch along the Mississippi River from Baton Rouge to New Orleans lined with refineries and petrochemical facilities next to residential areas, which has earned the sobering sobriquet "Cancer Alley," are witnessing more COVID-19 deaths than the rest of the country.

Of course, black Americans are at higher risk from COVID-19 for many reasons. We're more likely to be among the essential workforce keeping cities running and

> **As recently as April 14, the EPA rejected its own scientists' recommendation to restrict the very pollutants that the Harvard study says are increasing the COVID-19 death rate.**

grocery stores stocked during the pandemic, to live in more populated areas and to have less access to quality health care and food. We also suffer more than our share of the population from underlying illnesses that can exacerbate COVID-19, like obesity and diabetes, which often are diseases of poverty.

This has broken through, at least a bit. Some of the bus drivers and hospital orderlies dying of the virus, many of whom are African American, are making the news.

Air pollution isn't ready-made for cable news, yet it is proving deadly. We've long known this could happen. A 2003 study found a link between air pollution exposure and death from SARS, which is similar to the novel coronavirus, and air pollution is one culprit that the federal government could start taking steps to address now. We know what it takes at the policy level to cut air pollution, from supporting public transit to restricting emissions from power plants, to using cleaner fuels and energy sources.

Yet, since day one of his presidency, Donald Trump has ignored air pollution. He has spent three years loosening environmental regulations, doing more to line his friends' pockets than to save the economy or the lives of black folk.

Even during the pandemic, the Environmental Protection Agency under Trump is weakening critical safeguards for public health and choosing not to strengthen existing ones. As recently as April 14, the EPA rejected its own scientists' recommendation to restrict the very pollutants that the Harvard study says are increasing the COVID-19 death rate.

We cannot allow the daily press of crises to blind us to the environmental disaster that Trump is abetting and we cannot ignore the toll it is taking in this epidemic. We must demand that our government leaders address the environmental issues that unfairly impact our community.

But we're not hopeful that Trump can be moved to do the right thing. We haven't seen any indication from this administration righting any of the many wrongs of the past.

Print Citations

CMS: Dewese, Jared. "Black People Are Dying from the Coronavirus—Air Pollution Is One of the Main Culprits." In *The Reference Shelf: Pollution,* edited by Micah L. Issitt, 43-51. Amenia, NY: Grey House Publishing, 2020.

MLA: Dewese, Jared. "Black People Are Dying from the Coronavirus—Air Pollution Is One of the Main Culprits." *The Reference Shelf: Pollution,* edited by Micah L. Issitt, Grey Housing Publishing, 2020, pp. 49-51.

APA: Dewese, J. (2020). Black people are dying from the coronavirus—Air pollution is one of the main culprits. In Micah L. Issitt (Ed.), *The reference shelf: Pollution* (pp. 49-51). Amenia, NY: Grey Housing Publishing.

Trump Dismantles Environmental Protections under Cover of Coronavirus

By Emily Holden
The Guardian, May 11, 2020

The Trump administration is diligently weakening US environment protections even amid a global pandemic, continuing its rollback as the November election approaches.

During the Covid-19 lockdown, US federal agencies have eased fuel-efficiency standards for new cars; frozen rules for soot air pollution; proposed to drop review requirements for liquefied natural gas terminals; continued to lease public property to oil and gas companies; sought to speed up permitting for offshore fish farms; and advanced a proposal on mercury pollution from power plants that could make it easier for the government to conclude regulations are too costly to justify their benefits.

The government has also relaxed reporting rules for polluters during the pandemic.

Trump's ambitions reach even to the moon, which he has announced he wants the US to mine.

Gina McCarthy, formerly Barack Obama's environment chief, now runs the Natural Resources Defense Council. She said the Trump administration was acting to cut public health protections while the American public is distracted by a public health crisis.

"People right now are hunkered down trying to put food on the table, take care of people who are sick, worry about educating their children at home," McCarthy said. "How many people are going to really be able to sit down and scrutinize these things in any way?"

McCarthy said the government was "literally not interested in the law or science," and that "is going to become strikingly clear as people look at how the administration is handling Covid-19."

The Trump administration is playing both offense and defense, rescinding and rewriting some rules and crafting others that would be time-consuming for a Democratic president to reverse.

The Environmental Protection Agency (EPA) has written what critics say will be a weak proposal for climate pollution from airplanes, a placeholder that will hinder stricter regulation.

Trump officials have been attempting to create a coronavirus relief program for oil and gas corporations, a new move in his campaign to back the industry and stymie global climate action. The president has sown distrust of climate science and vowed to exit the Paris climate agreement, which the US can do after the election.

Historians say Trump's presidency has forced a pendulum swing back from the environmental awakening of the 1960s and 70s, when there was bipartisan support for conservation. Protecting the environment—and particularly the climate—is an issue that has become embroiled in political ideology.

"What Trump's done is create a blitzkrieg against the environment ... trying to dismantle not just Obama's environmental achievements but turn back the clock to a pre-Richard Nixon day," said Douglas Brinkley, a history professor at Rice University who is writing a book on the subject.

"It's just death by a thousand cuts. It's not one issue, it's just across the board."

The administration is under a tight deadline to secure changes before the election. A US law, the Congressional Review Act, allows lawmakers to more easily rescind regulations or rollbacks issued later in an election year.

"They're hitting a now or never timeline," said Christine Tezak, the managing director at the analysis firm ClearView Energy Partners. "There's a lot they want to get done before the election, just in case."

Some trends are working against Trump—including states advancing environmental goals, and low-cost renewable power and natural gas helping reduce the climate footprint of the electricity sector. Even Houston, an energy hub, has issued a climate action plan. Yet such contributions are not expected to be enough to fulfill America's role in stalling the global crisis.

Environmental advocates have challenged many of the Trump changes in court—and won. The Natural Resources Defense Council has sued 110 times and says it has prevailed in about 90% of lawsuits resolved.

Recently, judges tossed out a permit for the Keystone XL oil sands pipeline and decided the EPA cannot bar scientists who receive federal grants from serving as agency advisers.

Jeff Holmstead, a lawyer with the firm Bracewell who represents regulated industries and was a deputy EPA administrator under George W. Bush, argued that many of the changes characterized as "rollbacks" are actually "sensible, reasonable regulatory reforms" or fixes to problems.

"It's impossible to understand the Trump administration's EPA unless you go back and look at the Obama administration," he said. "In many groups there was a sense that there really had been a great deal of regulatory overreach. And even if you disagree with that, the regulatory programs created problems that they didn't come back and fix."

"This Is about Who We're Protecting"

Trump's deregulatory agenda has addressed some issues industry would rather were left alone. The agency is changing the way it calculates the benefits of mercury controls for power plants. Companies had already complied with the rule and most didn't want it changed. But the revision is meant to set a precedent for the

> **Protecting the environment—and particularly the climate—is an issue that has become embroiled in political ideology.**

government to ignore some positive health outcomes of regulation.

Trump's weakened standards often go against science too, critics say.

Last month, for example, the EPA decided not to tighten rules for soot pollution, refuting rebutting guidance from experts that more stringent standards would save lives. The EPA has also repopulated advisory boards with representatives from industry and conservative states and is trying to change what science it can consider when developing health protections.

If a Democrat takes the White House, it will take years to reverse some changes. Moving faster would require Democrats holding both chambers of Congress. Even then, industry would fight hard.

Christopher Cook, the environment chief for Boston, said Trump's efforts had been "incongruous with all the actions that major cities are taking."

"The thing I would ask most Americans to consider when they're supporting stronger regulation is that this isn't about what we're protecting against, this is about who we're protecting," Cook said, noting that places with more pollution are faring worse under the coronavirus pandemic.

"Covid has been a dry run for the climate crisis. We've seen the populations that Covid affects because it attacks the respiratory system. We can't continue with bad air in America."

Print Citations

CMS: Holden, Emily. "Trump Dismantles Environmental Protections under Cover of Coronavirus." In *The Reference Shelf: Pollution,* edited by Micah L. Issitt, 52-54. Amenia, NY: Grey House Publishing, 2020.

MLA: Holden, Emily. "Trump Dismantles Environmental Protections under Cover of Coronavirus." *The Reference Shelf: Pollution,* edited by Micah L. Issitt, Grey Housing Publishing, 2020, pp. 52-54.

APA: Holden, E. (2020). Trump dismantles environmental protections under cover of coronavirus. In Micah L. Issitt (Ed.), *The reference shelf: Pollution* (pp. 52-54). Amenia, NY: Grey Housing Publishing.

Fine Particle Air Pollution Is a Public Health Emergency Hiding in Plain Sight

By Douglas Brugge and James Lane
The Conversation, November 15, 2018

Ambient air pollution is the largest environmental health problem in the United States and in the world more generally. Fine particulate matter smaller than 2.5 millionths of a meter, known as PM2.5, was the fifth-leading cause of death in the world in 2015, factoring in approximately 4.1 million global deaths annually. In the United States, PM2.5 contributed to about 88,000 deaths in 2015—more than diabetes, influenza, kidney disease or suicide.

Current evidence suggests that PM2.5 alone causes more deaths and illnesses than all other environmental exposures combined. For that reason, one of us (Douglas Brugge) recently wrote a book to try to spread the word to the broader public.

Developed countries have made progress in reducing particulate air pollution in recent decades, but much remains to be done to further reduce this hazard. And the situation has gotten dramatically worse in many developing countries—most notably, China and India, which have industrialized faster and on vaster scales than ever seen before. According to the World Health Organization, more than 90 percent of the world's children breathe air so polluted it threatens their health and development.

As environmental health specialists, we believe the problem of fine particulate air pollution deserves much more attention, including in the United States. New research is connecting PM2.5 exposure to an alarming array of health effects. At the same time, the Trump administration's efforts to support the fossil fuel industry could increase these emissions when the goal should be further reducing them.

Where There's Smoke …

Particulate matter is produced mainly by burning things. In the United States, the majority of PM2.5 emissions come from industrial activities, motor vehicles, cooking and fuel combustion, often including wood. There is a similar suite of sources in developing countries, but often with more industrial production and more burning of solid fuels in homes.

Wildfires are also an important and growing source, and winds can transport wildfire emissions hundreds of miles from fire regions. In August 2018, environmental regulators in Michigan reported that fine particles from wildfires burning in California were impacting their state's air quality.

Most deaths and many illnesses caused by particulate air pollution are cardiovascular—mainly heart attacks and strokes. Obviously, air pollution affects the lungs because it enters them as we breathe. But once PM enters the lungs, it causes an inflammatory response that sends signals throughout the body, much as a bacterial infection would. Additionally, the smallest particles and fragments of larger particles can leave the lungs and travel through the blood.

> **The smallest particles and fragments of larger particles can leave the lungs and travel through the blood.**

Emerging research continues to expand the boundaries of health impacts from PM2.5 exposure. To us, the most notable new concern is that it appears to affect brain development and has adverse cognitive impacts. The smallest particles can even travel directly from the nose into the brain via the olfactory nerve.

There is growing evidence that PM2.5, as well as even smaller particles called ultrafine particles, affect children's central nervous systems. They also can accelerate the pace of cognitive decline in adults and increase the risk in susceptible adults of developing Alzheimer's disease.

PM2.5 has received much of the research and policy attention in recent years, but other types of particles also raise concerns. Ultrafines are less studied than PM2.5 and are not yet considered in risk estimates or air pollution regulations. Coarse PM, which is larger and typically comes from physical processes like tire and brake wear, may also pose health risks.

Regulatory Push and Pull

The progress that developed countries have made in addressing air pollution, especially PM, demonstrates that regulation works. Before the U.S. Environmental Protection Agency was established in 1970, air quality in Los Angeles, New York and other major U.S. cities bore a striking resemblance to Beijing and Delhi today. Increasingly stringent air pollution regulations enacted since then have protected public health and undoubtedly saved millions of lives.

But it wasn't easy. The first regulatory limits on PM2.5 were proposed in the 1990s, after two important studies showed that it had major health impacts. But industry pushback was fierce, and included accusations that the science behind the studies was flawed or even fraudulent. Ultimately federal regulations were enacted, and follow-up studies and reanalysis confirmed the original findings.

Now the Trump administration is working to reduce the role of science in shaping air pollution policy and reverse regulatory decisions by the Obama administration. One new appointee to the EPA's Science Advisory Board, Robert Phalen, a professor of medicine at the University of California, Irvine, is known for asserting that modern air is actually too clean for optimal health, even though the empirical evidence does not support this argument.

On Oct. 11, 2018, EPA Administrator Andrew Wheeler disbanded a critical air pollution science advisory group that dealt specifically with PM regulation. Critics called this an effort to limit the role that current scientific evidence plays in establishing national air quality standards that will protect public health with an adequate margin of safety, as required under the Clean Air Act.

Opponents of regulating PM2.5 in the 1990s at least acknowledged that science had a role to play, although they tried to discredit studies that supported the case for regulation. The new approach seems to be to try to cut scientific evidence out of the process entirely.

No Time for Complacency

In late October 2018, the World Health Organization convened a special conference on global air pollution and health. The agency's heightened interest appears to be motivated by risk estimates that show air pollution to be a concern of similar magnitude to more traditional public health targets, such as diet and physical activity.

Conferees endorsed a goal of reducing global deaths from air pollution by two-thirds by 2030. This is a highly aspirational target, but it may focus renewed attention on strategies such as reducing economic barriers that make it hard to deploy pollution control technologies in developing countries.

In any case, past and current research clearly show that now is not the time to move away from regulating air pollution that arises largely from burning fossil fuels, in the United States or abroad.

Print Citations

CMS: Brugge, Douglas, and James Lane. "Fine Particle Air Pollution Is a Public Health Emergency Hiding in Plain Sight." In *The Reference Shelf: Pollution,* edited by Micah L. Issitt, 55-57. Amenia, NY: Grey House Publishing, 2020.

MLA: Brugge, Douglas, and James Lane. "Fine Particle Air Pollution Is a Public Health Emergency Hiding in Plain Sight." *The Reference Shelf Pollution,* edited by Micah L. Issitt, Grey Housing Publishing, 2020, pp. 55-57.

APA: Brugge, D., & Lane, J. (2020). Fine particle air pollution is a public health emergency hiding in plain sight. In Micah L. Issitt (Ed.), *The reference shelf: Pollution* (pp. 55-57). Amenia, NY: Grey Housing Publishing.

3
Waste and Land Conservation

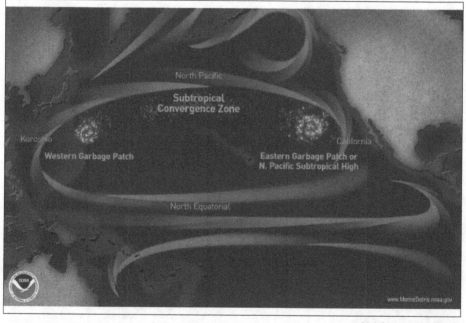

The Great Pacific Garbage Patch.

Wasted Lands

While clean air and water often receive the bulk of attention in discussions of pollution, the accumulation of solid waste and the pollution of soil are other major problems for which there are currently few solutions. Soil pollution and bulk waste also pose public health issues, but the problem has been less visible than air and water pollution. In the digital age, the problems of waste disposal and soil pollution have intensified, in large part due to the buildup of "e-waste," or "electronic waste," technological waste that has become a major problem in many American communities.

The Health of the Land

Soil is the substrate of human life. Soil is not simply lifeless mineral sediment, but a rich, living realm. There are billions upon billions of life-forms living within the soil, from subterranean insects and annelids to microscopic plants, fungi, and animals that infiltrate and enrich the terrestrial surfaces of Earth. The nutrients contained within the soil fuel the growth of plant, fungal, and animal life, and the death and decomposition of living things enriches the soil. Ancient humans, through observation and trial and error, discovered that they could collect and grow vegetables and fruits by transplanting seeds and plants into the soil. This discovery led to the birth of agriculture, the earliest signs of which have been found in ancient societies in what is now the nation of Iraq. By at least 11,000 years ago, humans were already learning to farm, and this meant learning about soil and what makes soil healthy for growing and living organisms.

Anthropologists have found evidence to suggest that individuals in the Mesopotamian civilization developed a system to rank the level of fertility between different types of soil, setting the stage for a rudimentary system of "soil science." These discoveries informed ancient Greek philosopher-scientists who wrote on different types of soil and the various minerals and substances that could be found within the Earth. Soil management became an established industrial and scientific art during the Greek civilizations of the ancient world, and records from ancient Egypt likewise suggest the beginnings of a complex science of agriculture and soil management, including techniques for fertilization and irrigation. For centuries soil science grew slowly, largely through the trial and error of farmers, but the scientific revolution in Europe brought new empirical research methods to the study of soil.[1]

In the Western canon of science, Russian scientist Vasily Vasilyevich Dokuchaev is considered the "father of soil science." Though Dokuchaev's study of the soil was dependent on earlier studies, such as now-famous research by German chemist Justus von Liebig, Dokuchaev created a formal classification of soil types and nutrients and helped to develop the study of soil into a subdiscipline of the natural sciences. He also pioneered the theory that the health of a sample of "Earth" was based on a holistic combination that included climate, living material within the soil, parent material (the ancient crushed rock and minerals that contribute to soil composition) and time.[2]

Another major leap from the scientific study of soil recognized that soil could become denuded and polluted thanks to human activity. When land is converted to create arable territory for planting crops or raising animals, plants are typically removed from the soil. When this happens, millions of microorganisms and fungi are also destroyed. Over time, and with repeated digging, turning, and treatment, soil does not actually improve but gradually loses nutrients and structure. These changes in soil composition and chemistry can have a dramatic impact on the environment. The now-famous disaster of the "Dust Bowl" contributed to the Great Depression. At the time, vast portions of the interior United States, known colloquially as "America's bread basket," had been converted into farmland to grow wheat and grain. As this occurred, trees, bushes, and other herbaceous plants were stripped from the plains, diminishing the integrity of the ecosystem. In 1930, the Great Plains region experienced the first of what became four major drought episodes, leading to water and food shortages. In 1935, major wind storms whipped through the region stirring the loose soil and dust into massive clouds that covered entire states, darkening the skies and making it nearly impossible for residents of the region to remain. Tens of thousands were forced to migrate out of the Great Plains. The Dust Bowl was the product of poor soil management, and the poor management of soil is something that continues to the present day.[3]

One positive aftershock of the Dust Bowl tragedy was the birth of soil conservation in American politics and agriculture. Much of this development was due to Hugh Hammond Bennett, a geologist and chemist now known as the "Father of Soil Conservation" for his pioneering work in establishing the basis of sustainable soil conservation practices and his role in helping to create the Soil Conservation Act of 1935, which led to the Soil Conservation Service being established as a new branch of the US Department of Agriculture (USDA). Bennett and many of the soil conservationists he inspired spent years working with farmers and communities to develop more sustainable practices, with mixed results. During the 1930s Americans first became widely aware of the fact that human activity could degrade and destroy the lithographic portion of the biosphere, and this was a step toward beginning to understand the practices that contribute to soil pollution.[4]

Land Use and Reclamation

The pollution of the soil began early in human history. One of the most destructive practices involving soil chemistry and stability is mining, which results in the physical destruction of the soil and also leads to industrial chemicals and byproducts being dumped into the soil. Pollutants also seep through soil and rock to reach waterways, bringing pollution into the water system. As humanity transitioned from an agrarian lifestyle to an industrial lifestyle pollution of the land intensified. In the 1800s, during the shift to industrialization, there were few if any laws across America regarding the disposal of waste. Factories and large-scale food production facilities dumped solid and liquid waste indiscriminately into soil and water systems. The demand for power to fuel the industrialized growth of American society then led to the birth of the fossil fuel industry. While humans had been burning coal and oil since antiquity, the advent of the combustion engine and later of the automobile greatly increased the demand for petroleum products. The result was a massive increase in mining and other invasive methods used to extract petroleum and coal and this led to a vast increase in soil and land pollution.

In some cases, especially when it comes to petroleum exploration and extraction, the waste produced can be extremely harmful to wildlife and human health; this is labeled hazardous waste. There are many kinds of hazardous waste, including that produced by mining, petroleum extraction and refinement, and the manufacture of pesticides and other chemicals. One specific type of toxic waste that requires special disposal and management is medical waste, which includes cleaning supplies, discarded gloves, needles, and other equipment that become infected with human tissues and potentially pathogens. In the late twentieth-century nuclear waste, the byproduct of generating nuclear energy, created a new kind of toxic waste problem. Many household products—cleaners, paints, solvents, motor oil, fluorescent lights, and aerosol products—also result in the accumulation of hazardous waste.[5]

It took quite some time for laws to catch up with the danger posed by hazardous waste. It wasn't until the late twentieth century that states and the federal government established regulations on the disposal of waste that poses a health risk to humans. The first serious laws weren't put into place until the 1950s, and it wasn't until the 1970s and 1980s that the federal government began to intervene to create rules for the disposal of potentially hazardous materials. For instance, laws regarding the establishment of landfills were not standardized to any serious extent until the passage of the Resource Conservation and Recovery Act (RCRA) of 1976. This law provides federal guidelines on the storage and disposal of waste and prohibits mismanagement that pollutes public or private land not set aside for waste disposal. The RCRA also specifically prohibits the dumping of hazardous waste except in areas specifically set aside for hazardous disposal. Further, the 1976 Congress passed the Toxic Substances Control Act to further regulate the creation and disposal of new chemicals. This law was meant to give environmental protection authorities, and specifically the Environmental Protection Agency (EPA), the power to control types of new and emerging chemicals being added to landfills.[6]

The consequences when hazardous waste is not well managed can be severe. In 1977, only a year after the federal government passed the RCRA, a spark from a welder's torch set in motion a series of chemical reactions that led to a massive fire at a chemical waste treatment plant in New Jersey, killing six and hospitalizing at least 35 as toxic smoke and fire tore through the facility. This facility is now one of hundreds of what are called "Superfund sites," named for 1980s legislation that attempted to set aside funding for the clean-up of the nation's most toxic and polluted areas. As of 2020, there are at least 40,000 Superfund sites across America. These are areas that have been set aside for investigation and remediation, but investigations have been pending on many of these areas since the 1980s. The Superfund program utilizes tax revenues but also seeks to identify and prosecute individuals and companies deemed to be responsible for polluting a specific site. For instance, Picher, Oklahoma, is an abandoned town destroyed by unregulated mining practices and slowly evacuated over the course of a century. The air, water, and soil in Pitcher remain deadly even decades after mining operations ceased.[7]

Unregulated mining is one of the greatest producers of hazardous waste. In the case of Pitcher, the corporations involved in harvesting the town's mineral resources are long gone and so remediation efforts need to be funded entirely by public resources. The purpose of EPA regulations on the disposal of hazardous waste is to ensure that companies profiting from activities that produce waste take responsibility for their activities and utilize their profits, rather than public resources, to appropriately manage the byproducts and pollution they create.

There are many examples, from across America and around the world, of toxic locations polluted through the activities of corporate negligence. Responsible management of resources, including the disposal of waste, presents a significant cost that can reduce corporate profitability. Corporations may therefore resist or even invest resources in fighting against waste disposal laws and policies. This strategy greatly reduces the effectiveness of environmental laws aimed at limiting the release of toxic chemicals, especially when companies can form alliances with politicians at the municipal, state, and federal levels. Donald Trump, who is personally invested in and has received financial support from at least a dozen companies linked to toxic waste production, has reduced funding for the EPA.

Reduction and Reuse

Although the environmental consciousness movement of the 1960s changed American attitudes about waste, pollution, and environmental protection, Americans have been unwilling to make environmental issues a serious priority. As a result, America does not rank highly among the world's nations in terms of sustainable development and the management of trash and waste. The growth of America's consumer-oriented culture has contributed greatly to this problem. As of 2020, the United States accounts for only 4 percent of the global population but produces 12 percent of the world's waste, meaning that Americans produce three times as much waste as the average world citizen. In comparison, China and India collectively account for 36 percent of the global population and both nations together contribute only 27 percent of the world's waste. Overproduction and indiscriminate disposal of waste is only one dimension of America's great trash problem, however, as the nation also sits well behind comparable nations in terms of progress in reusing and recycling materials. To give one of many examples, Americans recycle only about 30 to 35 percent of their waste, while Germany, the world's most efficient recycling nation, manages to recycle nearly 68 percent.[8]

As America's cities have fallen behind in terms of making progress on recycling and reducing waste, the problem has only grown more severe. In the twenty-first century a growing proportion of the waste produced by American homes and corporations is electronic waste, which contains nonbiogradable materials and toxic chemicals. The improper disposal and storage of e-waste has therefore become one of the most pressing issues in municipal waste management. In 2020, as Americans struggle through one of the least environmentally responsive governments, of the last half century, environmental activists at the municipal, state, and national level have been attempting to alert citizens to the severity of these deepening problems. As with air and water pollution, the accumulation of waste and the pollution of the soil are devastating for wildlife and natural ecosystems but also pose a serious threat to the health of the American people.

Works Used

"Basic Information about Landfills." *EPA*. 2020. https://www.epa.gov/landfills/basic-information-about-landfills.

Bradford, Alina. "Pollution Facts & Types of Pollution." *Live Science*. Feb. 28, 2018. https://www.livescience.com/22728-pollution-facts.html.

Brevik, Eric C. "A Brief History of Soil Science." *Land Use, Land Cover and Soil Sciences*. https://www.eolss.net/Sample-Chapters/C19/E1-05-07-01.pdf.

Holden, Emily. "US Produces Far More Waste and Recycles Far Less of It Than Other Developed Countries." *The Guardian*. July 3, 2019. https://www.theguardian.com/us-news/2019/jul/02/us-plastic-waste-recycling.

"Hugh Hammond Bennett." *Natural Resources Conservation Service*. USDA. https://www.nrcs.usda.gov/wps/portal/nrcs/detail/national/about/history/?cid=stelprdb1044395.

"The Most Toxic City in America." *Architectural Afterlife*. Jan. 15, 2019. https://architecturalafterlife.com/2019/01/15/the-most-toxic-city-in-america/.

Sweeney, Kevin Z. *Prelude to the Dust Bowl: Droughts in the Nineteenth-Century Southern Plains*. Norman: University of Oklahoma Press, 2016.

"Vasily Dokuhaev and Soil Science." *SciHi Blog*. Oct. 26, 2016. http://scihi.org/vasily-dokuchaev-and-soil-science/.

Notes

1. Brevik, "A Brief History of Soil Science."
2. "Vasily Dokuchaev and Soil Science," *SciHi Blog*.
3. Sweeney, *Prelude to the Dust Bowl: Droughts in the Nineteenth-Century Southern Plains*.
4. "Hugh Hammond Bennett," *Natural Resources Conservation Service*.
5. Bradford, "Pollution Fact & Types of Pollution."
6. "Basic Information about Landfills," *EPA*.
7. "The Most Toxic City in America," Architectural Afterlife.
8. Holden, "US Produces Far More Waste and Recycles Far Less of It Than Other Developed Countries."

60% of Superfund Sites Could Be Hit by Climate Change, New Government Report Finds

By Dino Grandoni and Brady Dennis
The Washington Post, November 18, 2019

At least 945 toxic waste sites across the country face escalating risks from rising seas, more intense inland flooding, voracious forest fires and other climate-fueled disasters, according to a new study from a congressional watchdog agency.

The report, published Monday by the Government Accountability Office, found that climate impacts threaten 6 in 10 Superfund sites overseen by the Environmental Protection Agency. GAO investigators said the agency needs to take more aggressive action to acknowledge risks facing some of the nation's most polluted sites—and to safeguard them amid a changing climate.

Even as they agreed with the GAO on certain points, Trump administration officials formally rejected a recommendation to clarify how preparing toxic sites to withstand the impacts of climate change is part of the EPA's mission.

"The EPA strongly believes the Superfund program's existing processes and resources adequately ensure that risks and any effects of severe weather events, that may increase in intensity, duration, or frequency, are woven into risk response decisions at non-federal [National Priorities List] sites," EPA Assistant Administrator Peter Wright said in a statement Monday.

The disagreement marks the latest instance of the Trump administration rejecting the warnings from independent researchers about the extent of the risk that rising global temperatures pose. Previously, the administration has downplayed government research about the potential severity of climate impacts in coming decades and aggressively rolled back Obama-era regulations aimed at reducing emissions of carbon dioxide.

"The report raises critical issues that are not being addressed," said Nancy Loeb, director of the Environmental Advocacy Center at Northwestern University's Pritzker School of Law, who was not involved in the GAO study. "It's a huge shortcoming not to take climate change into consideration."

The most common risk identified in Monday's GAO report is flooding. At least 783 sites around the country were found to have a great risk of inundation due to rainier conditions brought about by warming temperatures.

Among the locations found to have the highest flooding hazard is the Conservation Chemical site in Kansas City, Mo.

Already, that six-acre site has had to contend with epic Midwestern floods. When the Missouri River topped its bank in March, managers upped the pumping rate of the groundwater treatment system to contain dangerous chemicals buried underground.

How might managers at a flood-prone site prepare for climate change?

Mathy Stanislaus, a former EPA assistant administrator who oversaw the Superfund program under President Barack Obama, said in a phone interview that protective caps covering toxic waste may need to be made from different material—say, rubber liner instead of dirt—or may need to be built at steeper angles so water is less likely to collect atop sites and seep into the waste.

"This was a fairly significant concern of ours during the Obama administration," Stanislaus said, adding that officials concluded "that adaptation should be a core part of the standard operating practices for all of EPA's cleanup projects."

In particular, he said, sites near 100-year and 500-year flood plains, as well as those one meter or less above sea level, are "particularly at risk."

According to the report, 234 toxic sites are at high risk from wildfires, including a half dozen in California, where devastating blazes have become a deadly annual occurrence. And at least 187 properties in coastal states are vulnerable to storm surges brought by Category 4 and 5 hurricanes.

The GAO conducted the analysis at the behest of a group of mostly Democratic lawmakers, including presidential candidates such as Sens. Bernie Sanders (I-Vt.), Kamala D. Harris (D-Calif.) and Cory Booker (D-N.J.), who asked the congressional investigative arm to look into the issue in 2017.

After the release of the report, Senate Democrats sent a letter to EPA Administrator Andrew Wheeler demanding an explanation for agency leaders' "failure to embrace addressing climate change as a strategic objective."

"We believe that EPA's refusal to implement GAO's recommendations could result in real harm to human health and the environment as the effects of climate change become more frequent and intense," the lawmakers told Wheeler.

In 2014, the Obama-era EPA issued an agency-wide plan for adapting to climate change that included steps to be taken by the Superfund program.

> **Trump administration officials formally rejected a recommendation to clarify how preparing toxic sites to withstand the impacts of climate change is part of the EPA's mission.**

Since then, the agency has offered optional trainings on integrating climate change into the cleanup of sites. But on the ground, regional offices have inconsistently taken climate change into account. For example, EPA managers in the New York City area incorporated potentially stronger storm flows in the Passaic River in the remediation of a site in Newark. Yet regional EPA officials in Dallas, by contrast, told GAO they do not incorporate potential climate impacts into their assessments.

EPA spokeswoman Molly Block said the agency is in the process of implementing a "climate resilience action plan" at Superfund sites and has encouraged approaches that would allow specific sites to adapt to new and changing risks.

"The EPA recognizes the importance of ensuring Superfund site cleanups are resilient in the face of existing risks and extreme weather events and the agency has taken measures to include vulnerability analyses and adaptation planning into Superfund activities," the agency wrote in response to the GAO's findings.

While the Trump administration has rolled back Obama-era rules limiting carbon emissions from cars and coal plants and proposed cuts to Superfund funding, EPA leaders have also made a point of working to accelerate cleanup efforts at highly polluted sites.

Dozens of sites have been removed from the EPA's National Priorities List, and the agency maintains an ongoing "priority list" for sites most in need of attention.

"All Americans deserve timely action on Superfund site cleanups in their communities—not delays," Wheeler said in announcing updates to that priority list last month. "We will continue to advance or accelerate Superfund cleanups across the country by addressing issues that cause site-specific delays."

Print Citations

CMS: Grandoni, Dino, and Dennis Brady. "60% of Superfund Site Could Be Hit by Climate Change, New Government Report Finds." In *The Reference Shelf: Pollution,* edited by Micah L. Issitt, 67-69. Amenia, NY: Grey House Publishing, 2020.

MLA: Grandoni, Dino, and Dennis Brady. "60% of Superfund Site Could Be Hit by Climate Change, New Government Report Finds." *The Reference Shelf: Pollution,* edited by Micah L. Issitt, Grey Housing Publishing, 2020, pp. 67-69.

APA: Grandoni, D., & Brady, D. (2020). 60% of superfund site could be hit by climate change, new government report finds. In Micah L. Issitt (Ed.), *The reference shelf: Pollution* (pp. 67-69). Amenia, NY: Grey Housing Publishing.

Plastic Recycling Is Broken: Why Does Big Plastic Want Cities to Get $1 Billion to Fix It?

By Shannon Osaka
Grist, May 11, 2020

As the coronavirus pandemic cripples the U.S. economy, corporate giants are turning to Congress for help. Polluting industries have been among the first in line: Congress has already bailed out airlines, and coal companies have snagged over $30 million in federal small-business loans. Big Plastic is next in line with what might seem a surprising request: $1 billion to help fix the country's recycling.

A group of plastic industry and trade groups sent a letter to House Speaker Nancy Pelosi on April 16, asking Congress to allocate $1 billion to municipal and state recycling infrastructure in the next pandemic stimulus bill. It would be part of legislation known as the RECOVER Act, first introduced in Congress last November. Recycling sounds great, and has long been an environmental policy that almost everyone—Republicans and Democrats both—can get behind. To some environmentalists and advocates, however, the latest push is simply the plastic industry trying to get the federal government to clean up mountains of plastic waste in an attempt to burnish Big Plastic's image.

"Plastic recycling has been a failure," said Judith Enck, a former regional director for the Environmental Protection Agency and the founder of the organization Beyond Plastics. "And there's no reason to try to spend federal tax dollars to try to prop up plastic recycling when it really hasn't worked for the last 30 years anyway."

Put simply, very little of your plastic recycling actually gets recycled. According to the Environmental Protection Agency, less than 10 percent of the plastic produced in the past four decades has been recycled; the rest has wound up in landfills or been incinerated. In 2017, the U.S. produced over 35 million tons of plastic, yet less than 3 million tons was made into new products.

Part of the problem is that some items are composed of different types of plastic and chemicals, making them difficult to melt down and process. Only plastics with a "1" or "2" symbol are commonly recycled, and even then, they are more often "downcycled" into different types of products. A container of laundry detergent or a plastic soda bottle might be used for a new carpet or outdoor decking, but rarely into a new bottle. And downcycling is one step closer to the landfill. "The logo of recycling is the arrow that goes around and around—but that's never been the case with plastic," said Enck.

Big plastic-producing companies also have little incentive to use recycled materials rather than virgin materials. Plastics are made from petroleum, and when the price of crude oil is as low as it is now, it costs more to manufacture goods from recycled polymers than from crude.

Some analysts say that the RECOVER Act doesn't take on these larger issues. The act is aimed at the "curbside" aspect of recycling: funding city and state recycling collection, improving sorting at processing plants, and encouraging consumer education—teaching people what can (and cannot) go into recycling bins. (The legislation is also backed by the American Chemistry Council, which represents Dow Chemical and ExxonMobil, and has long fought against municipal plastic bag bans.)

There are some curbside problems with recycling. If plastic bags or containers covered with food waste get into recycling bins, they can contaminate other items and make sorting and reuse more difficult.

But Jonathan Krones, a professor of environmental studies at Boston College, said the real problem isn't at the curb. It's that "there aren't robust, long-term resilient end markets for recycled material." Even if cities manage to collect and sort more recycling, without markets all those perfectly processed plastics have nowhere to go.

For decades the U.S. solved part of the problem by selling hundreds of thousands of tons of used plastics to China. Then, in 2018, the Chinese government implemented its "National Sword" policy, forbidding the import of 24 types of waste in a campaign against foreign trash. The U.S. suddenly had lost the biggest market for its used plastics, and cities across the U.S. began burning recyclables or sending them to landfills. Some cities have stopped recycling plastic and paper altogether.

So why is Big Plastic pushing the RECOVER Act? Some argue that petroleum companies are trying to paper over the failures of plastic recycling. If consumers realized that only 10 percent of their plastics are ultimately recycled, they might push for bans on plastic bags and other single-use items, or more stringent restrictions on packaging. Keeping the focus on recycling can distract public attention from the piles of plastic waste clogging up our landfills and oceans. And a recent investigation by *NPR* and *Frontline* revealed that since the 1970s the plastics industry has backed recycling programs to buttress its public image.

> **Keeping the focus on recycling can distract public attention from the piles of plastic waste clogging up our landfills and oceans.**

"Had this bill been proposed 10 years ago, I think I would have said it was a good idea," Krones said, referring to the RECOVER Act. "But what has been revealed after National Sword is that this is not, by any stretch of the imagination, a technology problem. It's a consumption problem and a manufacturing problem." He argues that any attempt to fix plastic recycling should come with constraints on the production of new materials—only manufacturing plastics that can be easily broken down and reused, for example, or mandating that companies include a certain percentage of recycled materials in their products.

There are other ways to deal with the plastic problem. In February, Senator Tom Udall of New Mexico, a Democrat, introduced the Break Free from Plastic Pollution Act, which would phase out many single-use plastic items like utensils and straws and require big companies to pay for recycling and composting products—what's known as "extended producer responsibility." Other countries have similar laws on the books: Germany has required companies to take responsibility for their own packaging since 1991, and it's been credited with dramatically reducing waste.

For now, plastic use is on the rise. According to Rachel Meidl, a fellow in energy and environment at Rice University, the pandemic is bringing piles of takeout boxes and plastic bags to landfills, as cities ban reusable bags and enforce social distancing. She thinks that the RECOVER Act could be helpful, but that it needs to be coupled with other interventions.

"No matter how much government funding is allocated towards recycling efforts, there first needs to be a significant paradigm in human behavior," she said. "Where plastic is viewed as a resource, not a waste."

Print Citations

CMS: Osaka, Shannon. "Plastic Recycling Is Broken: Why Does Big Plastic Want Cities to Get $1 Billion to Fix It?" In *The Reference Shelf: Pollution,* edited by Micah L. Issitt, 70-72. Amenia, NY: Grey House Publishing, 2020.

MLA: Osaka, Shannon. "Plastic Recycling Is Broken: Why Does Big Plastic Want Cities to Get $1 Billion to Fix It?" *The Reference Shelf: Pollution,* edited by Micah L. Issitt, Grey Housing Publishing, 2020, pp. 70-72.

APA: Osaka, S. (2020). Plastic recycling is broken: Why does big plastic want cities to get $1 billion to fix it? In Micah L. Issitt (Ed.), *The reference shelf: Pollution* (pp. 70-72). Amenia, NY: Grey Housing Publishing.

Four Things You Didn't Know about Nuclear Waste

By Laura Leay
The Conversation, May 1, 2020

Some of what you've heard about nuclear waste is true. It really can take thousands of years to decay, and even the briefest exposure to the most dangerous kind can be lethal.

But in my ten years working with and researching nuclear waste, I've also encountered a lot of nonsense. It's simply not as bad as many of the scare stories make out. And with the UK and other countries having to decide where to host the next generation of nuclear waste disposal facilities, such misconceptions can be very damaging.

Nuclear waste can be thought of as anything that comes from a site licensed to handle nuclear material which is no longer useful. Radioactive waste is anything that isn't useful and also gives off harmful ionising radiation. I want to clear up a few things about these types of waste:

1. It doesn't glow.

This is not a documentary:

Homer Simpson's real-life equivalents are not constantly handling glowing objects.

If you could see into a nuclear reactor, or some cooling ponds that hold radioactive waste, you would indeed see a blue glow. But this isn't directly coming from the radioactive material.

The blue glow is given off by the water when charged particles, such as electrons, are emitted from the radioactive material at very high speeds. The water slows the charged particles down by absorbing some of their energy and the water then gives off this energy in the form of light. This makes the water around some radioactive objects appear to glow very brightly.

And if you thought the glow would be green rather than blue, this myth probably has its origins in the use of radioactive substances to make glow-in-the-dark paint.

In the 1920s, many so-called "Radium Girls" died in the US after licking paintbrushes in a factory where they worked applying glow-in-the-dark paint to watches.

---

2. It's not kept in oil barrels.

Popular images suggest barrels that look a little bit like they might contain oil. But waste from the nuclear industry takes many forms and there isn't much of it that actually looks like oil.

Some things are classified as radioactive waste because they're coated in dangerous radioactive particles that would be very difficult to remove. This includes things like filters from air vents and suits that workers have worn to stop the particles from getting on their skin. It also includes scraps of metal, sand used in water treatment processes, and rubble.

The really radioactive stuff comes from spent nuclear fuel, mostly uranium that has been used inside a reactor, some of which has undergone radioactive decay that converts it into different chemical elements. The spent fuel is dissolved in acid so that the useful chemical elements can be extracted and used to make new fuel.

The remaining liquid waste is then converted back into a solid (glass), which makes it easier to handle. This sort of waste doesn't take up much physical space, but accounts for most of the radioactivity in the UK inventory.

3. It's packaged to very high standards.

Most of the solid types of waste are placed into a 500 litre drum and then have a very specific type and amount of cement poured on top. This then flows around the waste and turns it into a strong and solid block that is pretty radiation resistant compared to other materials, like plastic.

Some types of waste are squashed in a specialist machine before cementation. Where liquid waste is turned in to glass, it must meet some quality criteria such as how much power it can give off from the radioactive isotopes. These criteria ensure the waste can be safely stored for a long time.

Some of it is so radioactive it gets hot. Used nuclear fuel contains lots of different radioactive elements

> The really radioactive stuff comes from spent nuclear fuel, mostly uranium that has been used inside a reactor.

and some of them decay very quickly. When they decay, they give off a lot of energy that can be absorbed by their surroundings, making them warm.

4. Some of it can be handled safely.

Radiation is all around us. It comes from the rocks in the ground, from space and from certain medical procedures such as X-rays.

If you experience a lot of radiation very quickly it will cause harm, but low amounts can be handled safely. This is why radiation workers have limits that they stick to. Someone who works with radiation is allowed to receive a dose of 20 millisieverts per year (a sievert is a measure of radioactivity). In comparison, a chest X-ray will give you a radiation dose of 0.1 millisieverts.

Print Citations

CMS: Leay, Laura. "Four Things You Didn't Know about Nuclear Waste." In *The Reference Shelf: Pollution,* edited by Micah L. Issitt, 73-75. Amenia, NY: Grey House Publishing, 2020.

MLA: Leay, Laura. "Four Things You Didn't Know about Nuclear Waste." *The Reference Shelf: Pollution,* edited by Micah L. Issitt, Grey Housing Publishing, 2020, pp. 73-75.

APA: Leay, L. (2020). Four things you don't know about nuclear waste. In Micah L. Issitt (Ed.), *The reference shelf: Pollution* (pp. 73-75). Amenia, NY: Grey Housing Publishing.

On Nuclear Waste, Finland Shows U.S. How It Can Be Done

By Henry Fountain

The New York Times, June 9, 2017

OLKILUOTO ISLAND, Finland—Beneath a forested patch of land on the Gulf of Bothnia, at the bottom of a steep tunnel that winds for three miles through granite bedrock, Finland is getting ready to entomb its nuclear waste.

If all goes well, sometime early in the next decade the first of what will be nearly 3,000 sealed copper canisters, each up to 17 feet long and containing about two tons of spent reactor fuel from Finland's nuclear power industry, will be lowered into a vertical borehole in a side tunnel about 1,400 feet underground. As more canisters are buried, the holes and tunnels—up to 20 miles of them—will be packed with clay and eventually abandoned.

The fuel, which contains plutonium and other products of nuclear fission, will remain radioactive for tens of thousands of years—time enough for a new ice age and other epochal events. But between the two-inch-thick copper, the clay and the surrounding ancient granite, officials say, there should be no risk of contamination to future generations.

"We are pretty confident we have done our business right," said Timo Aikas, a former executive with Posiva, the company that runs the project. "It seems the Olkiluoto bedrock is good for safe disposal."

The repository, called Onkalo and estimated to cost about 3.5 billion euros (currently about $3.9 billion) over the century or so that it will take to fill it, will be the world's first permanent disposal site for commercial reactor fuel. With the support of the local municipality and the national government, the project has progressed relatively smoothly for years.

That is a marked contrast to similar efforts in other countries, most notably those in the United States to create a deep repository in Nevada. The Yucca Mountain project, which would handle spent fuel that is currently stored at 75 reactor sites around the country, faced political opposition from Nevada lawmakers for years and was defunded by the Obama administration in 2012.

Now, with the backing of the nuclear power industry—and with the retirement of Yucca Mountain's chief nemesis, Senator Harry Reid of Nevada—the Trump administration wants to take the project out of mothballs. But its fate remains uncertain.

Experts in nuclear waste management say the success of the Finnish project is due in part to how it was presented to the people who would be most affected by it. Each community under consideration as a repository location was consulted and promised veto power should it be selected.

In the United States, Congress in 1987 pre-emptively directed that only Yucca Mountain be studied as a potential site, effectively overruling opponents in Nevada who were worried that the project might affect water supplies or otherwise contaminate the region.

"When you look at the Finnish repository, it's natural to admire the technical accomplishment," said Rodney C. Ewing, a professor at Stanford and former chairman of the Nuclear Waste Technical Review Board, an independent federal agency that reviews Energy Department programs, including Yucca Mountain. "But of equal importance has been the social accomplishment."

Mr. Aikas, who was involved in the Finnish site selection process beginning in the 1980s, said he and his colleagues learned early lessons about the need to consult with local residents.

"We ran into difficulties because we tried to behave as industry did back then— we'd decide and announce," he said. Invariably, he said, by presenting decisions as unreviewable, they ran into local opposition.

"Very soon we learned that we had to be very open," Mr. Aikas added. "This openness and transparency creates trust." When five sites were selected for further study in 1987, offices were opened in each community to provide information.

The approach proved so successful that when it came time for the national government to make a final decision on a repository in 2000, officials in Eurajoki, the municipality that includes Olkiluoto Island, agreed to host it on one condition: that Posiva not present the government an option to choose any other site.

Eurajoki officials had concerns early in the process, Mr. Aikas said, but eventually came to see that the repository would provide property tax revenue and jobs.

The municipality also had experience with nuclear power: Two of the country's four operating nuclear power reactors are on Olkiluoto, less than two miles from the repository, and a third plant is under construction nearby.

"You have a community that is familiar with nuclear issues," said Dr. Ewing at Stanford.

Nevada, by contrast, has no nuclear power plants. What it does have is a history of government testing of atomic weapons, both in the air and underground, for four decades until the early 1990s.

"You have to expect that a community with that experience will be a little skeptical," Dr. Ewing said.

Finland's success also has its roots in an early decision by the national government. In 1983, it established the principle that the companies creating the waste— TVO, which owns the reactors at Olkiluoto, and Fortum Power and Heat, which owns the other two—are responsible for disposing of it. The government had only approval and regulatory roles.

The government had only approval and regulatory roles.

"It has always been important to resolve this spent-fuel issue and keep it in the hands of the power company," Mr. Aikas said. Posiva, the company developing the repository, is a joint venture of the two utilities.

In the United States, spent fuel became the responsibility of the federal government, specifically the Energy Department, subjecting the issue to more political pressures.

At the Onkalo site, workers drill into the bedrock down near the 1,400-foot level, taking cores to study the characteristics of the granite. Above ground, near the curving entrance to the tunnel, construction has begun on a building where the spent fuel, currently cooling in pools at the Olkiluoto reactors, will be readied for burial, handled by remote-controlled machinery since radiation levels will be high. Spent fuel will also eventually be shipped here from Fortum's reactors, on the country's southeastern coast.

Kimmo Kemppainen, research manager for the project, said that in characterizing and mapping the rock, it was important to locate, and avoid, fractures where water could flow, since the disposal site was below the water table. But even if water gets near a canister, he said, the clay should form a barrier and keep corrosion of the copper—which could result in a radiation leak—to a minimum, even over tens of thousands of years.

Mr. Kemppainen has worked on the project for 14 years. "My personal opinion is that for this generation that has used nuclear power, at least we should do something about the waste," he said. "It's not safe to store it on the surface."

> The repository, called Onkalo and estimated to cost about 3.5 billion euros (currently about $3.9 billion), will be the world's first permanent disposal site for commercial reactor fuel.

In the United States, more than 80,000 tons of spent fuel are currently stored on the surface, in pools or dry steel-and-concrete casks, at operating nuclear reactors and at other sites near now-closed plants. The original deadline to have a repository operating by 1998 is long past.

The project at Yucca Mountain, in the Mojave Desert about 100 miles northwest of Las Vegas, has been studied for years at a cost of more than $13 billion. In 2008, the Energy Department began the process of obtaining a construction license from the Nuclear Regulatory Commission. But the Obama administration moved to withdraw the license application two years later.

With the election of President Trump, advocates for Yucca Mountain saw a chance to revive it.

"This is a very important national project," said Rod McCullum, a senior director at the Nuclear Energy Institute, an industry group. "If we can do this safely, we would be ashamed of ourselves if we didn't do it."

The Trump administration is seeking $120 million to reopen the licensing process. And in a symbolic gesture, in his first official trip as energy secretary, Rick Perry toured the site, where little exists beyond a five-mile-long exploratory tunnel.

Congress rejected the licensing funds in its deliberations on the 2017 budget, and the 2018 budget process is just starting. Even if the $120 million is allocated, it could take a half-decade or longer, and much more money, to complete the licensing, which would involve a lengthy hearing before administrative judges on hundreds of environmental and safety issues raised by opponents.

Even without Mr. Reid, most members of Nevada's congressional delegation are still vowing to fight the project, arguing that there are concerns about the long-term safety of drinking water supplies—unlike the Finnish repository, the Nevada site sits above the water table—and that above all, Nevadans do not want it.

The decision to put the repository there "was based on bad politics, not good science," said Representative Dina Titus, a Democrat who represents a Las Vegas district.

"The main issue is consent," she said. She and other members of the delegation have introduced a bill that would require the host state's approval before the repository could be built.

In a 2012 report, an expert panel established by the Obama administration to develop a new strategy for managing spent fuel recommended a similar consent-based process. It had another Finland-like recommendation as well: that responsibility for nuclear waste be taken from the Energy Department and put in the hands of an organization created solely for that purpose.

Those recommendations have not been acted upon. But it is also unclear whether Yucca Mountain, if revived by the Trump administration, would succeed under the current approach.

"It could be that the federal government could prevail and after some decades we would have a repository," Dr. Ewing said. "It could be that after several decades the federal government could fail and we would be where we are at today."

There's a lot to be said for how Finland handled its situation, Dr. Ewing added. "If you treat people fairly and present them the information, if the repository is safe, you should be able to get some communities to respond positively," he said.

Print Citations

CMS: Fountain, Henry. "On Nuclear Waste, Finland Shows U.S. How It Can Be Done." In *The Reference Shelf: Pollution,* edited by Micah L. Issitt, 76-79. Amenia, NY: Grey House Publishing, 2020.

MLA: Fountain, Henry. "On Nuclear Waste, Finland Shows U.S. How It Can Be Done." *The Reference Shelf: Pollution,* edited by Micah L. Issitt, Grey Housing Publishing, 2020, pp. 76-79.

APA: Fountain, H. (2020). On nuclear waste, Finland shows U.S. how it can be done. In Micah L. Issitt (Ed.), *The reference shelf: Pollution* (pp. 76-79). Amenia, NY: Grey Housing Publishing.

How a Nuclear Stalemate Left Radioactive Waste Stranded on a California Beach

By Rachel Becker

The Verge, August 28, 2018

When I got to the San Onofre State Beach about 60 miles north of San Diego, the red sun of fire season was sandwiched on the horizon between a layer of fog and the sea. Surfers floated in a line off the shore. It looked like any other California beach—except for the row of signs that warned "Nuclear Power Plant Exclusion Area," and the twin reactor domes rising above the bluffs.

I was there to see the San Onofre Nuclear Generating Station, a shuttered nuclear power plant right next to the Pacific Ocean. It once supplied electricity to Southern California, but was permanently shut down in 2013. It's now scheduled to be dismantled, but even when that happens, more than 1,700 tons of spent nuclear fuel will remain—interred in enormous concrete casks behind a seawall. There's nowhere else to put it.

"It's Part of the Landscape Now."

On the beach, perspectives on the plant ranged from resignation to frustration. "It's part of the landscape now," said one man walking his dog. A woman who was roasting marshmallows in the sand with her family said it's eerie to see the plant when she's out surfing: "You turn around and take a wave, and you just see these nuclear boobs staring out at you." Her husband wondered what will happen with the spent nuclear fuel now that the plant is no longer operating. "No citizen wants it here permanently, but nobody wants to take it," he said. "So we're just in a really hard spot. What are you supposed to do with it?"

It's a question that nuclear power plants around the country are reckoning with as low natural gas prices, costly repairs, and political pressure have driven a half dozen reactors to retire early since 2013, according to the Department of Energy. More are slated to shut down in the next ten years—including Diablo Canyon, California's last nuclear power plant, Rob Nikolewski reports for the *San Diego Union-Tribune*. That leaves communities that are no longer benefiting from nuclear power saddled with its waste—cooling off in gigantic pools of water made out of reinforced concrete or steel and concrete containers called dry storage.

All those containers of fuel left behind mean that no one can use the land for anything else. And the problem is widespread: spent fuel from commercial reactors is scattered across roughly 80 sites in 35 different states, according to the Government Accountability Office. It wasn't supposed to be like this: for decades, the plan has been to bury highly radioactive nuclear waste underground. (There were also proposals to bury the waste in the ocean or shoot it into the sun—but those weren't as practical, according to a report by the Blue Ribbon Commission on America's Nuclear Future.)

The idea is that a geologic repository would keep the waste away from people as the radioactivity decays—which can take hundreds of thousands of years, depending on the material. In the 1980s, the government settled on Yucca

> **All the containers of fuel left behind mean that no one can use the land for anything else.**

Mountain in Nevada as the most likely spot and planned to start taking shipments of spent nuclear fuel in 1998. In return, the deal was that utilities—really, their customers—would start paying ahead into a fund that would cover the costs. But Nevada politicians like Senator Harry Reid (D-NV) hated what became known as the "screw Nevada bill," and the project has hit delay after delay ever since.

"We're Just in a Really Hard Spot. What Are You Supposed to Do with It?"

Now, utilities like Southern California Edison, which operated San Onofre, are stuck in a holding pattern: guarding the waste, and suing the government for billions of taxpayer dollars to pay for it. "The federal government has not fulfilled their obligation to come take the fuel from this plant site, or any commercial plant site," Ron Pontes, team manager of decommissioning environmental strategy at San Onofre, told me. "So, until they do so, the fuel is here and we are charged with taking care of it."

Verge Science's video team and I went on a tour of the plant to see what it means to take care of that fuel. First, though, we had to get through security. That meant gearing up with hard hats and safety glasses, signing off that we hadn't had alcohol in past five hours, and taking our boots off to go through an airport-style security portal. Then came another stop to have our hands scanned and get buzzed through metal turnstiles and into the protected area.

Once staffed by roughly 2,200 people, there are now just a few hundred working on-site, including security personnel. And outside on the pavement encircled by metal fences, the place felt empty. Except for the seagulls, the sound of the waves, and the occasional concussive booms from the neighboring US Marine Corps Base Camp Pendleton, it was quiet.

Our guide was Pontes, the decommissioning team manager, a white-haired 61-year-old in a blue button-up whose career started on nuclear submarines in the Navy. He led us into a dark, red metal building tangled with pipes and metal tubes, and then into an elevator. There were only four cryptic buttons for the floors labeled 9, 30, 50, and 70—for the number of feet above sea level. We went to 70, the top of the structure housing the massive metal turbines. Those don't turn anymore: "The turbine is just so much iron now," Pontes says. "It serves no purpose."

"The Turbine Is Just So Much Iron Now. It Serves No Purpose."

From there, we could look out to see a white buoy floating in the ocean, marking the end of massive tubes that sucked in seawater to cool the plant. The dome of the Unit 3 reactor building towered behind us. Powered up in the 1980s, Units 2 and 3 are mirror images of each other. (Unit 1 was dismantled in 2008.) Inside those grey concrete domes, uranium atoms split in a chain reaction to produce heat. "That's the business end of this operation," Pontes says. "That's where the heat is generated that is transmitted to the steam generators, makes steam to turn the turbines, which makes electricity for our customers."

He used present tense—but the plant hasn't made electricity in years. Not since a steam generator in the Unit 3 dome sprung a leak in 2012. These days, Southern California Edison is preparing to decommission the plant—a $4.4 billion process that's anticipated to take 20 years. First, though, they had to move the bundles of nuclear fuel rods from the reactor cores into Olympic-sized, steel-lined cooling pools. (We didn't get to see them, but Pontes says that the crystal-clear water looks "very inviting to swim in.")

By the middle of 2019, the plan is to shift all of the fuel into steel containers encased in massive concrete blocks. Called dry storage, it's air-cooled so it's lower maintenance than the pools: it's designed to keep the radioactive fuel from overheating without using water, pumps, or electricity. These concrete monoliths are supposed to hold up against floods, earthquakes, tornadoes—even an airplane collision, according to the Nuclear Regulatory Commission. The dry storage comes in two flavors on the San Onofre site: in one, the canisters stand up vertically in the steel-lined cavities of a massive concrete block; in another, they slide in horizontally, like corpses into a nuclear morgue.

With so few people at the plant, nature was making a comeback: on our way to the dry storage, our security escort had to hang back to call in a swarm of bees that had colonized a piece of equipment. Pontes imagined what the future of the plant will look like, when it's finally decommissioned. "At the end of the day, all that's left here is the dry storage facility and the security officers that will be monitoring this facility," he said. And both could be there for awhile.

A Swarm of Bees Had Colonized a Piece of Equipment

There are a few possible fixes. Two different private companies have applied to the Nuclear Regulatory Commission for licenses to construct interim storage facilities in Texas and New Mexico. But the key word there is interim: these sites would be temporary holding areas for fuel that will eventually move to a permanent repository—like Yucca Mountain, the controversial site in Nevada that's about 100 miles northwest of Las Vegas, and across the state line from Death Valley in California.

At first, the list of possible long-term repositories for highly radioactive waste was longer than just Yucca Mountain. Hanford in Washington state and Deaf Smith County in Texas also rose to the top, according to a report by the Blue Ribbon Commission on America's Nuclear Future. Plus, there were supposed to be two repositories, so that one state wouldn't be stuck with an entire nation's nuclear waste. "And then the idea was you couldn't do this quick and dirty, you'd spend several years and a billion dollars at each of those three sites," says Robert Halstead, executive director of Nevada's Agency for Nuclear Projects.

But the selection process dragged out, grew expensive, and none of those states were happy about being at the top of that particular list. So in 1987, Congress decided to just pick one site for the DOE to investigate: Yucca Mountain. The DOE "put a five-mile tunnel through the mountain, and did the science, and concluded this is a good place," says Lake Barrett, who headed up the Department of Energy's Office of Civilian Radioactive Waste Management at the time, and is now retired. He called it "the most studied piece of real estate on Earth."

Nevada objected to the DOE's conclusions—but Congress overrode that veto and in 2002, Congress and the president gave the DOE their blessing to apply to the Nuclear Regulatory Commission, or NRC, for a license to start construction. Pretty much as soon as the NRC began officially reviewing the application in 2008, the whole thing started grinding to a halt.

"The Most Studied Piece of Real Estate on Earth."

By then, Harry Reid (D-NV) was the Senate majority leader—and he opposed shoving "nuclear waste down a community's throat," he said in a statement in 2015. Barack Obama had campaigned on promises to prevent Yucca Mountain from opening, and once he took office, the funding for it dried up. After the DOE tried unsuccessfully to withdraw its licensing application in 2010, the operation mostly shut down. "People who used to work for me, they were all laid off," Barrett says.

Since then, the NRC's technical staff completed *part* of the licensing process when it issued its safety evaluation report in 2015. But the commission hasn't restarted the hearings necessary to weigh stakeholder concerns about the project—and it would need to, if Yucca Mountain were ever to become a nuclear waste repository. Now, a bill introduced by John Shimkus (R-IL) that passed the House in May proposes to clear the way for the licensing to proceed and would authorize interim storage facilities. It would let Nevada negotiate compensation in return for hosting the repository, ensure the DOE has the land rights it needs for the site, and increase the amount of waste that could be stored in the Yucca Mountain repository.

The bill probably won't get anywhere. "Historically, the Senate's not going to move," Shimkus said in an interview with *The Verge*. Senator Dean Heller (R-NV) called the bill "dead on arrival" in the Senate. But Shimkus says the bill shows the House's collective support for funding Yucca Mountain. That's key as the House and the Senate haggle over the budget for fiscal year 2019. "We're waiting to see how this final dance happens," Shimkus says.

Halstead, over at Nevada's Agency for Nuclear Projects, said, "The bill is a declaration of war on the state of Nevada." There are two big things wrong with it, according to Halstead: "They think that they can force this down Nevada's throat, and they're not going to be able to—and secondly, they think the Department Of Energy can carry out the program," he says, adding that the state of Nevada can "whup the Department of Energy. So bring it on."

"They Think That They Can Force This Down Nevada's Throat."

Nevada's skepticism about Yucca Mountain is understandable, says Rod Ewing, a professor of geological sciences at Stanford University. For one thing, there were some 100 nuclear devices exploded in the air above Nevada. "They were told it was safe. Didn't turn out quite that way," he says. Plus, Ewing says, "They don't have nuclear power plants, but you're asking them to take the waste?"

Yucca Mountain wouldn't be his first choice for a repository, either. "I'm not saying that it's *not* safe," Ewing says. But he also argues that it doesn't "satisfy the common sense requirements of a geologic repository." For example, in the 1990s, scientists found signs that water may percolate through the rock faster than expected. And the most likely way for radiation to escape the repository would be by hitching a ride with flowing water.

But other research groups have had trouble replicating those results. And Barrett pushes back, saying that very little water flows, it won't get into rivers or the ocean, and the waste containers are designed to prevent what goes into Yucca Mountain from getting out. "You can make these arguments to justify whatever your political motivation might happen to be," Barrett says.

The thing is, we know that progress toward an underground nuclear repository *is* possible—just look at Finland, which could start filling its underground repository with waste in the next decade, according to Timo Äikäs, a retired geologist who worked on the project. And Äikäs has an idea about why it's so far ahead. There are a few hurdles to clear in order to build a geologic repository, he says. The first is to make sure the site is safe. "Today, in all countries which have operated nuclear power stations for several decades, there is lots of knowledge about these safety requirements," he says.

"The Program Is Running, and Running, and Running, and Nothing Happens."

The second, "which is much more tricky," Äikäs says, is convincing people to accept it. And that's where other countries have stalled. "Everything boils down to trust," Äikäs says. Without it, he says, "there will be no decisions, or the decisions will be postponed—and then the program is running, and running, and running, and nothing happens."

That's what's happening here in the US, and it's getting to the point where the government has to make a call about Yucca Mountain, because the clock is ticking, Shimkus says. "If the decision is that it's not safe, then we have to start the process all over again—that means another 30 years and another, at minimum, $15 billion," Shimkus says.

Until Yucca Mountain, interim storage, or an entirely new site are ready, the waste is going to sit where it was generated. None of the experts I spoke to are worried that radioactive fuel in dry storage could endanger people nearby. "There have not been any leaks of radiation from a dry cask in this country," Neil Sheehan, a spokesperson for the NRC, said in an email.

But recent mishaps at San Onofre have sparked local concerns. A loose pin in a new type of fuel canister raised alarm bells about faulty manufacturing. Southern California Edison stopped using those particular containers, and there have been no signs of trouble in the few that had already been filled with waste, Southern California Edison spokesperson Julie Holt told me. More recently, another fuel canister jammed on its way down into the concrete vault and could have fallen, Rob Nikolewski at the *San Diego Union-Tribune* reported. "If this had occurred, it would not have created a hazard to the public or employees," Tom Palmisano, vice president of decommissioning, said in a letter that was shared with *The Verge*.

"We Agree That It's Better to Move the Fuel Away from This Site, Okay?"

Still, the presiding sentiment among the people I spoke to is that keeping the waste at San Onofre, or any other plants across the country, is not a workable long-term plan. "The challenges here over the long term, the very long term, is that the sea level is rising," Pontes, our guide at the San Onofre plant, said to us in front of one of the dry storage blocks that stretched toward the sandy bluffs. That means that eventually, the fuel might have to move to higher ground. "We agree that it's better to move the fuel away from this site, okay?" he said. "But, while it's here, we will fulfill our obligation to manage it safely."

Pontes took us to the top of the newest dry storage monolith—the one where the canisters sit upright, and circulate air through chimney-like vents. We weren't allowed next to the canisters with fuel in them. Those were blocked off by rope, and radiated heat in shimmering waves. Eventually, there will be 73 filled spent fuel canisters encased in concrete, plus two containers that will be left empty. One of those will be heated to mimic the presence of fuel, to monitor how the canisters weather over years in the salty air.

Pontes walked us along the line of concrete lids for the empty fuel containers, and told us how robust the system is: three feet of reinforced concrete in the foundation. Two feet of reinforced concrete at the top. And sandwiched in between? More concrete. I wondered what that meant for earthquakes—and Pontes told me that the concrete block is supposed to withstand even bigger earthquakes than the plant was designed to take. What about tsunamis? "The analyzed tsunami is much lower than the seawall," he said. "If this were to be swamped, you could have 125 feet of water above the top of these cylinders." After a flood, they'd pump out the water, clean off the canisters, and continue operating, he said.

"Eventually, It Becomes Untenable."

But nature is coming for the spent fuel canisters in ways their designers may not have anticipated—in the form of seagulls, and their poop. When the plant was operating, the seagulls liked to nest on the warm containment buildings, Pontes says. "Once we shut down and there were fewer people on-site and less activity, they seem to have returned—in a big way."

Now, the dry storage lids are splattered with droppings. To be clear, the poop won't endanger the fuel. But to keep the birds from getting too comfortable, fake coyotes stand guard amid the canisters of nuclear waste and snarl from the tops of plastic traffic cones. They're keeping the dry storage as seagull-free as they can until the Department of Energy is ready to pick up the fuel. Pontes thinks that will have to happen, one day: "Eventually, it becomes untenable," he says. "The problem that we have with this fuel being here is a problem that exists almost everywhere."

On our way out of the plant, we ran a Geiger counter over our hands and feet. It clicked as it checked us for radiation. We were fine.

Print Citations

CMS: Becker, Rachel. "How a Nuclear Stalemate Left Radioactive Waste Stranded on a California Beach." In *The Reference Shelf: Pollution,* edited by Micah L. Issitt, 80-86. Amenia, NY: Grey House Publishing, 2020.

MLA: Becker, Rachel. "How a Nuclear Stalemate Left Radioactive Waste Stranded on a California Beach." *The Reference Shelf: Pollution,* edited by Micah L. Issitt, Grey Housing Publishing, 2020, pp. 80-86.

APA: Becker, R. (2020). How a nuclear stalemate left radioactive waste stranded on a California beach. In Micah L. Issitt (Ed.), *The reference shelf: Pollution* (pp. 80-86). Amenia, NY: Grey Housing Publishing.

4
Side Effects

By NASA Earth Observatory images by Joshua Stevens, using Suomi NPP VIIRS data from Miguel Romàn, NASA's Goddard Space Flight Center.

In addition to interfering with viewing the night sky, light pollution has had a deadly impact, through disrupting normal behavior patterns, for many species. Above, a composite image of the continental United States at night (2016).

Hidden Dimensions

In many ways, pollution that is less obvious than littering and the accumulation of physical waste poses a hidden problem. Deadly chemicals that seep into the air and leech into the water supply are often invisible, and thus the dangers posed by pollution can be insidious. In many cases, it is only when illness has spread among a community, or when ecologists or outdoor enthusiasts notice a loss of biodiversity, that communities become aware of hidden substances circulating through their environment. However, while air, water, and land pollution have remained at the forefront of environmental consciousness, there are many other ways in which humanity pollutes its environment. Two of the lesser-known ways are flooding the environment with unnatural sources of light and creating tremendous amounts of noise. Both noise and light pollution have been shown to pose a grave threat to wildlife, disrupting migratory and seasonal patterns and interfering with climatic cycles that animals depend on to navigate their world. In addition, both noise and light pollution have been shown to have demonstrable impact on humans and have been linked to a variety of mental and physical health issues.

Too Much Light

Light pollution—artificial light produced by human societies—can alter the environment in ways that can be dangerous for biological life. The problem of light pollution did not attract significant attention until the mid-twentieth century when professional and amateur astronomers reported that light from cities and towns was making it impossible or difficult to see familiar constellations and other astrological objects in the night sky. Within a short time, studies from biological research were beginning to show how deeply light pollution can impact animal populations, sometimes with disastrous results.

The history of how humans learned to harness the power of light is long and complex, and stretches back to the Paleolithic discovery of fire. Fire is not a technological innovation but rather a naturally occurring part of the environment. Natural fires typically occur in areas where lightning ignites trees or other plants, and most wildfires occur in grasslands, prairies, or dry forests. Humans are believed to have evolved in the savannahs of East Africa, which is still an ecosystem favorable to the spread of wildfires, and it is likely that these annual fire events were what first introduced fire to humanity. Fires could be moved and extended by obtaining burning remains and using those embers to ignite other dried materials. Studies suggest that the control of fire likely began before the evolution of humanity, when *Homo erectus* lived in Africa. Anthropologists have found evidence of human-controlled fire in the area around Lake Turkana in Kenya, including oxidized patches of earth several inches deep indicating that the population of *Homo erectus* were maintaining and utilizing fire. However, there is no evidence that humans were regularly creating and using fire until between 400 to 800,000 years ago. Anthropologists studying this period have found evidence of regular fire usage in communities ranging from Africa to Europe. Fire was a transformative discovery, enabling humans to survive climate conditions that would otherwise be unlivable and settle in near arctic regions.[1]

While fire provided heat and the ability to cook food, it also allowed the extension of work and other activities beyond the reach of the sun. In the eighteenth century, sustainable lighting using burning gas was developed. This was more practical than burning wood or coal and enabled municipalities to install permanent lighting. Kerosene lamps and lanterns became popular in the early 1900s and were installed in American homes and cities around the 1930s. The next development was the "arc lamp," which created light by passing a charge through two electrodes in a gas-filled chamber. Then, in 1879 Thomas Edison's patent for the incandescent light bulb dramatically changed the world.[2] The incandescent light bulb works by passing an electric current through a thin metal filament; when the filament becomes heated it lets off a glow. Other ways of producing light were gradually discovered through the twentieth century, including the use of neon (a reactive gas), fluorescent lighting, and eventually digital lighting through light- emitting diodes (LEDs). As the human population grew, and the technology used to control light advanced, the nighttime world became a brighter and brighter place, but this development ultimately had unintended consequences.

The brains of humans and other animals are not designed to exist in constant light. The physiological systems of the body, and often various kinds of behavior, are tuned to the regional light-dark cycle of the region where a species first evolved. The day-night cycle determines when certain species are active and when they sleep. Sleep is an essential part of the day for nearly all creatures, providing an opportunity for cells and organ systems to conduct important maintenance activities that keep bodies and minds working. For instance, without sleep, humans rapidly begin exhibiting symptoms of psychological stress, including paranoia and hallucinations. Further, fatigue limits energy, strength, and endurance. Even after only 24 hours without sleep, an average human will exhibit a mental state comparable to a blood alcohol level of 0.10 percent, which is beyond the capacity for legally operating a motor vehicle.[3] Research has shown that darkness is an important component of sleep and one of the side effects of an "over lit" world may therefore be increased incidents of insomnia and other sleep disorders.

For nonhuman animals, the impact of an artificially illuminated world can be even more disastrous. A number of species have evolved to be active in the dark, and may navigate using cues that are difficult to follow in environments polluted by artificial light. Researchers have found, for instance, that artificial lights from cities and towns can disrupt the navigation patterns of hundreds of bird species that typically utilize the position of the moon and stars at night. Light pollution makes these cues more difficult to detect and may also cause birds and other nocturnal animals to follow false cues. Light pollution has also endangered some species, most famously by affecting the migration of sea turtles. Many species of sea turtle are born on land after their parents climb onto the shore to bury their eggs in sand. The hatching of the babies is timed to occur at night, when temperatures are lower and there are fewer predators around. After emerging from their nests, young turtles are hardwired to head toward the brightest light they perceive. Before humanity, this would always mean the light of moon, which would lead them back to sea. However, human coastal cities create so much light that baby turtles frequently become confused and sometimes head toward the city, where thousands die each year from automobiles and other hazards.[4]

In comparison to air, water, and land pollution, the issue of light pollution has only begun to gain widespread attention from researchers and urban planners, and there are movements in a number of countries to darken environments or, at least, to find ways to help animals coexist in humanity's light-polluted environment. Ultimately, light pollution is another challenge that must be met if humanity is ever to reach the goal of establishing green cities.[5]

Silent Nights

Another way in which humanity has unwittingly altered the environment in a detrimental way is by creating noise. Noise pollution refers to loud or inescapable noises that fill an environment. There are many different sources, and all pose a health issue for humans and other species. Unlike light pollution, there are a number of laws already in place in American towns and cities that specifically address noise pollution. In many areas, it is illegal to conduct construction work or to make other loud noises during hours when many people are sleeping. Many towns and cities have enacted laws against loud music and other noise disturbances. There is also a system in place to address noise pollution at the federal level through the Clean Air Act Title IV, which was established during the 1990 amendments to the Clean Air Act and specifically covers noise pollution. Title IV defines noise pollution as "unwanted or disturbing sound," and prohibits such noise when it "interferes with normal activities such as sleeping, conversation, or disrupts or diminishes one's quality of life."[6] Noise from ground and air traffic, construction, loud music, and a variety of industrial activities are often cited as examples.[7]

The 1990 noise pollution amendment was the result of numerous studies documenting how excessive noise impacted people and other animals. Direct links were found between excessive noise and such health conditions as high blood pressure, hearing loss, and other physiological issues. A study from the European Environment Agency (EEA) released in March of 2020 opined that noise pollution may contribute to 48,000 new cases of ischemic heart disease and as many as 12,000 premature deaths each year. Heart disease and other blood pressure issues are related to the way in which noise pollution causes continued annoyance and stress, and the EEA estimates that noise pollution may be a contributing factor in at least 22 million cases of "high annoyance" and 6.5 million cases of chronic sleep disturbance documented each year. Further, the EEA estimates that noise from air traffic might be a factor in the reading impairment experienced by more than 12,000 school children.[8]

Noise pollution is even more detrimental to nonhuman animals, especially those dependent on hearing for navigation, communication, and finding food. Bats and owls, common nocturnal predators throughout North America, both rely on auditory signals to find food and to navigate their environments. Noise from human activity can mask other noises disrupt their ability to find food. Researchers have also found that many kinds of birds use auditory clues when navigating or migrating, and excessive noise can likewise disturb migratory and navigational patterns.

Engineers and scientists are already looking into ways to reduce common contributors to noise pollution. For instance, as of 2020 there is research underway to potentially eliminate the noise of emergency sirens by sending siren sounds directly to internet radio systems inside of vehicles. Another example can be found in the Environmentally Responsible Aviation Project from National Aeronautics and Space Administration (NASA), which has been looking into ways to reduce the environmental noise caused by air traffic using a variety of methods, from installing hybrid engines to repositioning engines to the top of the plane's wings to reduce noise transmitted to the ground.[9]

Noise and light are but two of the many ways that human life and culture impacts the natural world and poses threats to human and animal health. Solving problems like noise and light pollution are important factors toward creating sustainable societies that can exist in equilibrium with the environment.

Works Used

"Animals Need the Dark." *NPS*. National Park Service. Apr. 19, 2018. https://www.nps.gov/articles/nocturnal_earthnight.htm.

Biggers, Alana, and Jamie Eske. "The Effects of Going More Than 24 Hours without Sleep." *Medical News Today*. Mar. 26, 2019. https://www.medicalnewstoday.com/articles/324799.

"Clean Air Act Title IV—Noise Pollution." *EPA*. 2020. https://www.epa.gov/clean-air-act-overview/clean-air-act-title-iv-noise-pollution.

Eschner, Kat. "Is Light Pollution Really Pollution?" *Smithsonian*. June 1, 2017. https://www.smithsonianmag.com/smart-news/light-pollution-really-pollution-180963474/.

Goines, Lisa, and Louis Hagler. "Noise Pollution: A Modern Plague." *Southern Medical Journal*. Vol. 100, Mar. 2007.

Hirst, K. Kris. "The Discovery of Fire." *Thought Co*. May 4, 2019. https://www.thoughtco.com/the-discovery-of-fire-169517.

Mason, Betsy, and Keith Axline. "A Brief History of Light." *Wired*. Dec. 25, 2000. https://www.wired.com/2008/12/gallery-lights/.

Peris, Eulalia. "Noise Pollution Is a Major Problem, Both for Human Health and the Environment." *European Environment Agency*. June 8, 2020. https://www.eea.europa.eu/articles/noise-pollution-is-a-major.

Semuels, Alana. "The Future Will Be Quiet." *The Atlantic*. Apr. 2016. https://www.theatlantic.com/magazine/archive/2016/04/the-future-will-be-quiet/471489/.

Notes

1. Hirst, "The Discovery of Fire."
2. Mason and Axline, "A Brief History of Light."
3. Biggers and Eske, "The Effects of Going More Than 24 Hours without Sleep."
4. "Animals Need the Dark," *NPS*.
5. Eschner, "Is Light Pollution Really Pollution?"
6. "Clean Air Act Title IV—Noise Pollution," *EPA*.
7. Goines and Hagler, "Noise Pollution: A Modern Plague."
8. Peris, "Noise Pollution Is a Major Problem, Both for Human Health and the Environment."
9. Semuels, "The Future Will Be Quiet."

Is Noise Pollution the Next Big Public-Health Crisis?

By David Owen

The New Yorker, May 6, 2019

I worried about ringing the doorbell. Then I noticed two ragged rectangles of dried, blackened adhesive on the door frame, one just above and one just below the button. I deduced that the button had been taped over at some point but was now safe to use. I pressed as gently as I could, and, when the door opened, I was greeted by a couple in their early sixties and their son. The son has asked me to identify him only as Mark, his middle name. He's thirty years old, and tall and trim. On the day I visited, he was wearing a maroon plaid shirt, a blue baseball cap, and the kind of sound-deadening earmuffs you might use at a shooting range.

Mark and I sat at opposite ends of a long coffee table, in the living room, and his parents sat on the couch. He took off his earmuffs but didn't put them away. "I was living in California and working in a noisy restaurant," he said. "Somebody would drop a plate or do something loud, and I would have a flash of ear pain. I would just kind of think to myself, Wow, that hurt—why was nobody else bothered by that?" Then everything suddenly got much worse. Quiet sounds seemed loud to him, and loud sounds were unendurable. Discomfort from a single incident could last for days. He quit his job and moved back in with his parents. On his flight home, he leaned all the way forward in his seat and covered his ears with his hands.

That was five years ago. Mark's condition is called hyperacusis. It can be caused by overexposure to loud sounds, although no one knows why some people are more susceptible than others. There is no known cure. Before the onset of his symptoms, Mark lived a life that was noise-filled but similar to those of millions of his contemporaries: garage band, earbuds, crowded bars, concerts. The pain feels like "raw inflammation," he said, and is accompanied by pressure on his ears and his temples, by tension in the back of his head, and, occasionally, by an especially disturbing form of tinnitus: "You and I would have a conversation, and then after you'd left I'd go upstairs and some phrase you had been saying would repeat over and over in my ear, almost like a song when they have the reverb going." He manages his condition better than he did five years ago, but he still lives with his parents and doesn't have a job. The day before my visit, he had winced when his father crumpled a plastic cookie package that he was putting in the recycling bin. By the end of our conversation, which lasted a little more than an hour, he had put his earmuffs back on.

Hyperacusis is relatively rare, and Mark's case is severe, but hearing damage and other problems caused by excessively loud sound are increasingly common world-wide. Ears evolved in an acoustic environment that was nothing like the one we live in today. Daniel Fink—a retired California internist, whose own, milder hyperacusis began in a noisy restaurant on New Year's Eve, 2007, and who is now an anti-noise activist—told me, "Until the industrial revolution, urban dwellers' sleep was disturbed mostly by the early calls of roosters from back-yard chicken coops or nearby farms." The first serious sufferers of occupational hearing loss were probably workers who pounded on metal: blacksmiths, church-bell ringers, the people who built the boilers that powered the steam engines that created the modern world. (Audiologists used to refer to a particular high-frequency hearing-loss pattern as a "boilermaker's notch.")

Today, the sound source that people first think of when they think of hearing loss is amplified music, the appeal of which may be biological. In 1999, two scientists at the University of Manchester, in England, conducted an experiment in which they had students listen to songs at dance-club volumes, which are high enough to cause permanent damage if the exposures are long enough. The scientists concluded that the loud music stimulated the parts of the subjects' inner ears that govern balance and spatial orientation, thereby creating "pleasurable sensations of self-motion": crank up the volume, and you feel as though you're dancing when you're sitting in your seat. Classical musicians and their audiences face risks as well. For the musicians, the threat comes not just from their own instrument (violinists, like right-handed infantrymen, tend to lose hearing on their left side first) but also, often more significant, from the instruments of the musicians who sit behind them.

Modern sound-related health threats extend far beyond music, and they affect more than hearing. Studies have shown that people who live or work in loud environments are particularly susceptible to many alarming problems, including heart disease, high blood pressure, low birth weight, and all the physical, cognitive, and emotional issues that arise from being too distracted to focus on complex tasks and from never getting enough sleep. And the noise that we produce doesn't harm only us. Scientists have begun to document the effects of human-generated sound on non-humans—effects that can be as devastating as those of more tangible forms of ecological desecration. Les Blomberg, the founder and executive director of the Noise Pollution Clearinghouse, based in Montpelier, Vermont, told me, "What we're doing to our soundscape is littering it. It's aural litter—acoustical litter—and, if you could see what you hear, it would look like piles and piles of McDonald's wrappers, just thrown out the window as we go driving down the road."

In February, Bruitparif, a nonprofit organization that monitors environmental-noise levels in metropolitan Paris, published a report that combined medical projections from the World Health Organization with "noise maps" based partly on data from its own network of acoustic sensors. It concluded, among many other things, that an average resident of any of the loudest parts of the Île-de-France—which includes Paris and its surrounding suburbs—loses "more than three healthy life-years," in the course of a lifetime, to some combination of ailments caused or exacerbated by the din of cars, trucks, airplanes, and trains. These health effects, according to guidelines published by the W.H.O.'s European regional office last year, include tinnitus, sleep disturbance, ischemic heart disease, obesity, diabetes, adverse birth outcomes, and cognitive impairment in children. In Western Europe, the guidelines say, traffic noise results in an annual loss of "at least one million healthy years of life."

The headquarters of Bruitparif is in a low-rise office complex in Saint-Denis, a suburb just north of the Eighteenth Arrondissement. I visited a couple of weeks after the February report was issued, and met with Fanny Mietlicki, who has been Bruitparif's director since 2005. She had warned me, before my trip, that she spoke very little English. I, on the other hand, speak French almost as well as my father did. He studied it in school, and was stationed in France at the end of the Second World War. Years later, at a restaurant in Paris, while travelling with my mother, he said something to a Frenchman sitting at the next table, and the Frenchman said something back. Neither man could understand the other, and my mother eventually identified the problem: the Frenchman didn't realize that my father was speaking French, and my father didn't realize that the Frenchman was speaking English.

> **Hyperacusis can be caused by overexposure to loud sounds, although no one knows why some people are more susceptible than others. There is no known cure.**

Mietlicki's English turned out to be better than she'd let on. "You need to have data in order to know where to implement noise-abatement actions," she told me. "Before Bruitparif, politicians were fighting to get money to construct noise barriers, but not necessarily where the most people live." In 2014, Bruitparif was one of the principal creators of the Harmonica index, a way of presenting the severity of sound disturbances with a simple graph. Harmonica's most appealing feature is that it makes no reference to decibels, which even acousticians have trouble explaining. (Part of the difficulty—but only part—is that decibels are logarithmic. A hundred-decibel sound isn't twice as intense as a fifty-decibel sound; it's a hundred thousand times as intense.)

Bruitparif's director of technology is Christophe Mietlicki, Fanny's husband. He used to develop computer systems for financial institutions, but, in 2009, he decided that his wife's job was more interesting than his, and went to work for her. They are in their forties, have three children, and commute each day from Suresnes, a suburb directly across the Seine from the Bois de Boulogne. At the headquarters, Christophe and I spoke in a sort of reception-and-recreation area on the floor below Fanny's office. On one of the walls was a large noise map of Paris and its suburbs, on which roads, train lines, and airline flight paths had been highlighted in angry, glowing red, like inflamed nerves in an ad for a pain reliever. On a wooden table in front of the map was a white bowl that was filled with what appeared from a distance to be individually wrapped pieces of candy but turned out to be earplugs.

We stepped into an adjacent room. "Here is our acoustic laboratory," Christophe said. He handed me one of Bruitparif's sound-monitoring devices, which he had helped invent. It's called Medusa. It has four microphones, which stick out at various angles, hence the name. The armature that holds the microphones is bolted to a metal box roughly the size of an American loaf of bread. Inside it is a souped-up Raspberry Pi—a tiny, inexpensive computer, which was originally intended for use in schools and developing countries but is so powerful that it has been adopted, all over the world, for myriad other uses. (You can buy one on Amazon for less than forty bucks.) Embedded in the central microphone stalk are two tiny fish-eye cameras, mounted back to back, which record a three-hundred-and-sixty-degree image each minute. Medusas are the successors of Bruitparif's first-generation sensors, called Sonopodes, which rely on expensive components imported from Japan. Sonopodes are still in use, although they are too big to move around easily. "The Japanese system is very good, but each one costs almost thirty thousand euros, and we can't deploy it as much as we expect," Christophe told me. "So we built our own system, which is small and low-cost. The idea is the same." Bruitparif has installed fifty Medusas in the metropolitan area, and will add many more this summer.

In a nearby room, a young woman was assembling Medusa microphones from components that were spread out on a counter. Most of the parts had been 3-D-printed, and she was doing something to some of them with what looked like a soldering iron. "In fact, it's very simple," Christophe said. "And, as with many things that are very simple, finding the solution was very complex." The orientation of the microphones on a Medusa enables it to pinpoint the origins of the sounds that it monitors; the cameras preserve time-stamped images of the scene. Bruitparif can place a Medusa on a street lined with noisy bars and, later, document precisely which bar, at what time, was playing music, say, eleven decibels louder than the local code allows.

I said that documentation like that would be useful in New York, where the police often ignore noise complaints or respond to them days later.

"The idea of this system is not to depend on the police," Christophe said. "That should be the last resort. We prefer a system in which people like you, like me, can put a sensor somewhere and have objective data, and then we can talk with one another and find some solution together."

Ah, *mais oui*. (But the data would probably also stand up in court.)

A few weeks later, back in the States, I visited the headquarters of a smaller but similar noise-monitoring project, at N.Y.U.'s Center for Urban Science and Progress, on Jay Street, in Brooklyn. That project is called Sounds of New York City (SONYC) and is funded mainly by the National Science Foundation. SONYC's purpose, Mark Cartwright, one of the scientists on the project, told me, is "to monitor, analyze, and mitigate noise pollution." Each sensor in its network has just one microphone, which is roughly eight inches long and covered in foam. The microphone is attached to a small, weatherproof aluminum box, which also contains a Raspberry Pi. Sometimes the sensors are mounted with a long strip of plastic spikes, which are meant to deter pigeons from using the devices as latrines, and which, on monitors installed near Washington Square Park, have developed the unanticipated additional function of accumulating tangled masses of the wind-borne hair of N.Y.U. students.

The method that SONYC uses to collect data and to document noise-code violations is different from the one used by Bruitparif. The SONYC researchers are developing algorithms that they hope will eventually be able to identify a full range of noise sources by themselves—an example of so-called machine listening. "Having a network of sensors deployed around the city enables us to start understanding the patterns of noise and how they develop around things like construction sites," Charlie Mydlarz, another scientist on the project, told me. He said that SONYC also gives the city's Department of Environmental Protection actionable evidence of violations. Mydlarz and his colleagues are still training their algorithm, with help from "citizen scientists," who visit a Web page and annotate ten-second audio files, collected by the sensors, with what they think are the sounds' likeliest sources: jackhammer, car alarm, chainsaw, engine of uncertain size. He demonstrated the algorithm's current iteration by alternately operating a Black & Decker electric drill and the siren of a toy fire truck near a sensor on the table in front of him. The algorithm successfully identified each and measured its decibel level. (It can also identify the fire truck's horn.)

I was accompanied to the SONYC lab by Charles Komanoff, an economist who created models that the city's congestion-pricing plan is based on. In the course of the past five decades, he's worked on just about every environmental issue, including noise. "In the mid-nineties, I spoke fairly regularly to small but spirited anti-car gatherings," he told me. "I would ask for a show of hands: 'If you could eliminate all motor-vehicle noise or all motor-vehicle air pollution—but not both—which would you choose?' As a rule, the majority chose noise." I had asked him to join me mainly because he owns a professional sound-level meter.

Komanoff and I travelled to and from Brooklyn by bicycle, and halfway across the Manhattan Bridge we stopped to take sound readings. His meter showed that, at the spot where we were standing, the average ambient-sound level, arising mostly from motor traffic on the bridge, was about seventy decibels, or roughly what you'd experience while using a vacuum cleaner at home. Then a train went over the bridge, on tracks twenty or thirty feet from where we were standing, and the reading jumped to ninety-five decibels—more than a three-hundredfold increase in sound intensity and a five- to sixfold increase in perceived loudness—or roughly what you'd hear while using a gasoline-powered lawnmower in your yard. The train sound wasn't physically painful, but almost; even shouted conversation became impossible.

In the United States, sound exposure in the workplace has been regulated by the federal government since the nineteen-seventies. But the rules don't cover all industries, and they're applied inconsistently. The government has acknowledged that, even when compliance is absolute, the limits aren't low enough to protect all workers from hearing loss. The regulations of the Occupational Safety and Health Administration, for example, allow workers to be exposed to ninety-five decibels for four hours a day, five days a week, for an entire forty-year career. That's always been crazy, but in the past decade it's begun to seem even crazier, because recent research into what's known as hidden hearing loss—which involves a previously undetected permanent reduction in neural response—has suggested that catastrophic losses could occur at sound levels that are much lower than had been thought, and after much shorter periods of exposure.

By the mid-nineties, some scientists had begun to believe that traffic noise must be harmful to creatures other than humans, but they didn't know how to measure its effects in isolation from those of roadway construction, vehicle emissions, highway salting, and all the other direct and indirect ecosystem insults that arise from our dependency on cars and trucks.

In 2012, Jesse Barber, a professor at Boise State University, in Idaho, thought of a way. He and a group of researchers built a half-kilometre-long "phantom road" in a wilderness area where no real road had ever existed. They mounted fifteen pairs of bullhorn-like loudspeakers on the trunks of Douglas-fir trees, and, during bird migration in autumn, played recordings of traffic that Barber had made on Going-to-the-Sun Road, in Glacier National Park. Chris McClure, who worked on the project, told me, "We cut up garden hoses to run the wires through, so that mice wouldn't chew on them, and we duct-taped pieces of shower curtains over the loudspeakers, to keep off the rain." The recorded sound wasn't deafening, by any measure; to a New Yorker, in fact, it might have seemed almost soothing. But its effect on migrating birds was both immediate and dramatic. During periods when the speakers were switched on, the number of birds declined, on average, by twenty-eight per cent, and several species fled the area entirely. Some of the biggest impacts were on species that stayed. Heidi Ware Carlisle, who earned her master's degree for work that she did on the project, told me, "If you just counted MacGillivray's warblers, for example, you might say, 'Oh, they're not bothered by noise.' But when we weighed them we found that they were no longer getting fatter—as they should have been, because fat fuels their migration."

A dozen years before the phantom-road experiment, a group of American researchers accidentally performed a similar study underwater. They had been measuring concentrations of stress-related hormone metabolites in the feces of right whales in the Bay of Fundy. (They were assisted by dogs trained to detect the scent of whale turds from the side of a boat.) In mid-September, 2001, the metabolite concentrations fell; when they were measured again the following season, they had gone back up. The scientists had been using hydrophones to monitor underwater sound levels in the bay, and they realized that the drop in stress had coincided exactly with an equally sudden decline in human-generated underwater noise. The cause was the temporary pause in ocean shipping which followed 9/11.

"His monogram says it all."

I learned about the Bay of Fundy project from Peter Tyack, an American behavioral ecologist, who, for the past seven years, has been a member of the faculty at the University of St. Andrews, in Scotland. He also does research at the Woods Hole Oceanographic Institution, on Cape Cod, where he used to work full time—and that's where we met. We sat in a lab on the second floor of W.H.O.I.'s Marine

Research Facility, and he explained that sound can harm marine creatures both directly, by physically injuring them, and indirectly, by interfering with their feeding, their mating, and their communication. "We're visual creatures, but sea animals don't need to be," he said. "Underwater, you can see maybe ten metres, but you can hear things a thousand kilometres away." The loudest human sounds in the oceans are made by seismic air guns, which are used to search for undersea deposits of oil and natural gas. (They're so loud that acoustic monitors on the Mid-Atlantic Ridge pick them up from hundreds, and even thousands, of miles away.) "In terms of the total sound energy that humans put into the ocean, though, shipping is by far the biggest source," he said.

Tyack gave me a tour of the research facility downstairs. We passed a bank of freezers, a room with a CT scanner, and a band saw big enough to carve a small whale into chunks, and then entered a room that was furnished with supersized versions of the kind of stainless-steel tables you'd find in the autopsy room of a morgue. "There's a big door over there, so that a truck can back right up," he said. "And those gantries up on the ceiling move the animals onto the tables."

One of Tyack's ongoing research interests is the impact of sonar on marine mammals. He and his colleagues have developed a sound-and-movement monitor—"sort of a waterproof iPhone"—which they can affix, with suction cups, to whales' backs. They have discovered, among other things, that some species are more sensitive to sonar than anyone had previously suspected. "If they hear sonar, they'll stop foraging, leave the area, and not come back for several days," he said. Sometimes frightened whales bolt toward the surface and die of decompression sickness—the bends—or of an arterial gas embolism. He continued, "We are now quite sure that what happens is that the whales are a kilometre deep, and they're foraging in the dark for food, and the sound of sonar from a naval exercise triggers a panic reaction."

Tyack said that it's long been known that human-created sound can also interfere with mating calls, thereby reducing the reproductive success of many species, including ones that have already been hunted virtually to nonexistence. Consequent reductions in those species' numbers can be invisible even to marine biologists, since the failure to reproduce doesn't result in carcasses on beaches. "Even now, our estimates of the population size of marine mammals are plus or minus fifty per cent," he said. "So, basically, the population would have to be on its way toward extinction before we'd notice. And by then it would be too late."

On the day that Charles Komanoff and I took those sound readings on the Manhattan Bridge, I also visited Arline Bronzaft, a retired professor of environmental psychology, at her apartment, on East Seventy-ninth Street, near the river. In 1975, she and a co-author published an influential research paper that, like the phantom-road and whale-poop studies, hinged on an accidental discovery. "One of my students, at Lehman College, told me that her child attended an elementary school next to an elevated train line, and that the classroom was so loud that the students were unable to learn," she said. The school was P.S. 98, in Inwood, near the northern tip of Manhattan, and the track was two hundred and twenty feet from the building. Bronzaft's student said that she and some other parents were planning to sue, but Bronzaft, whose husband was a lawyer, told her that, in order to be success-ful, they would need to prove that their children had been harmed. Bronzaft offered to help and found that, in classrooms on the side of the building facing the tracks, passing trains raised decibel readings to rock-concert levels for roughly thirty sec-onds every four and a half minutes, and that, during those periods, teachers had to either stop teaching or shout; then, once a train had passed, they had to regain their students' attention. Bronzaft obtained three years' worth of reading-test scores from the school's principal—"I must say, he was an activist principal," she said—and was able to demonstrate to the city that the sixth graders on the track side of the build-ing had fallen about eleven months behind those on the quieter side.

Bronzaft stayed involved. She helped persuade the city to cover the classroom ceilings with sound-deadening acoustic tiles, and the M.T.A. to install rubber pads between the rails and the ties on tracks near the school (and, eventually, throughout the subway system). In a follow-up study, published in 1981, she was able to show that those measures had been effective and that the gap in test scores between stu-dents on the exposed and less exposed sides of the building had disappeared.

Those experiences increased Bronzaft's impatience with scientists and politi-cians who hesitate to act on persuasive but incomplete data. She asked me if I knew who had been the President of the United States at the time of the passage of the federal Noise Control Act and of the establishment of the Environmental Protec-tion Agency, the Occupational Safety and Health Administration, and the National Institute for Occupational Safety and Health. And I did know: Richard Nixon. She took me into her office, a book-filled study that she calls the Noise Room, and, on a couch, opened an accordion folder that contained a dozen or so U.S.-government pamphlets, most of them from the seventies. One described noise impacts identical to the ones that researchers all over the world still study today, including hearing loss, cardiovascular disease, interrupted sleep, and delayed reading and language development. It concluded with a quotation from William H. Stewart, who served as the Surgeon General under both Lyndon B. Johnson and Nixon. In his keynote address at the 1968 Conference on Noise as a Public Health Hazard, in Washing-ton, Stewart said, "Must we wait until we prove every link in the chain of causa-tion?" and added, "In protecting health, absolute proof comes late. To wait for it is to invite disaster or to prolong suffering unnecessarily."

That was half a century ago. Scientists still don't know everything there is to know about the effects of sound on living things, but they know a lot, and for a long time they've also known how to make the world substantially less noisy. Peter Tyack told me that reducing the sound impact of global shipping would be possible, since "the navies of the world have spent billions of dollars learning how to make ships quiet." One method, he said, is to physically isolate engines from metal hulls; another is to shape propellers in ways that make them less likely to produce shock waves in the water. Subway cars everywhere could roll on rubber tires, as some of the ones I rode in Paris do. Highway speed limits could be enforced; so could laws requiring the use of E.P.A.-approved exhaust systems on all motorcycles. Maxi-mum earbud volumes could be limited to indisputably safe levels. Directional sirens could significantly reduce or eliminate noise for people who are not in the path of an emergency vehicle. Measuring noise is important, Bronzaft said, but it isn't an end in itself. "If I don't see the data being used to get action, I'm not going to be happy," she continued. "We had all this stuff in the nineteen-seventies. And what have we done?"

Print Citations

CMS: Owen, David. "Is Noise Pollution the Next Big Public-Health Crisis?" In *The Reference Shelf: Pollution,* edited by Micah L. Issitt, 95-103. Amenia, NY: Grey House Publishing, 2020.

MLA: Owen, David. "Is Noise Pollution the Next Big Public-Health Crisis?" *The Reference Shelf: Pollution,* edited by Micah L. Issitt, Grey Housing Publishing, 2020, pp. 95-103.

APA: Owen, D. (2020). Is noise pollution the next big public-health crisis? In Micah L. Issitt (Ed.), *The reference shelf: Pollution* (pp. 95-103). Amenia, NY: Grey Housing Publishing.

Noise Pollution Hurts Wildlife, but States Have Trouble Turning Down the Volume

By Alex Brown

PEW Stateline, October 22, 2019

PUGET SOUND, Wash.—A low rumble thrums through the deck as Tacoma, a 5,000-ton ferry, makes its run across Puget Sound from Seattle to Bainbridge Island. Standing near the railing, Colin McCann, a legislative analyst for Washington State Ferries, points to the water where the agency recently dropped a microphone 500 feet below the surface as part of a study to capture the acoustic profile of every vessel in the state's fleet.

Washington aims to protect the area's southern resident killer whales. The endangered clan of 73 orcas became a regional cause célèbre last summer after a grieving mother orca carried the body of her dead calf for 17 days.

The orcas track salmon using echolocation, or sonar, and research has shown that the din in these heavily trafficked waters has hampered their ability to detect prey. Reducing vessel noise was a key recommendation of the Orca Task Force assembled last March by Democratic Gov. Jay Inslee.

"There's been a lot of quick action," McCann said. "You've seen that urgency."

Once officials know the noise level each of the seven classes of ferries emits at various speeds, the agency will pair the details with a recently launched orca-tracking app. Ferry captains will be directed to slow down or reroute to accommodate the orcas.

Washington state also wants to quiet the discord affecting Olympic National Park, a landscape of coastal and mountain wilderness west of Seattle. Washington Attorney General Bob Ferguson, a Democrat, is suing to prevent the U.S. Navy from increasing flights over the park, citing effects on both nearby residents and wild animals, including endangered species.

These issues have made Washington one of the rare states to recognize sound pollution as a threat to its wildlife. Increasingly, research shows that human-caused noise can be harmful to many species. But very little regulation—and even less enforcement—exists in the United States to limit the increasing encroachment of noise on the environment.

"The literature has shown that noise fundamentally changes behavior, distributions and reproductive success [for wildlife]," said Jesse Barber, who runs the

Sensory Ecology Lab at Boise State University. "We can now clearly say that noise is a pollutant, but that takes some time to work its way into policy."

Washington state Sen. Christine Rolfes, a Democrat, said she expects the issue to gain visibility.

"It might be one of the next frontiers of pollution regulations," she said. "I don't know that people have ever thought of noise as pollution. I certainly wasn't that aware of it until recently."

Most local noise ordinances address nuisance noise in residential areas, the kind of racket that draws neighbors' complaints and has been shown to harm human health. Fewer legal guidelines exist to protect wildlife.

But states wanting to address the problem face challenges. Noise doesn't stop at state, county or city boundaries. Many of the loudest sources are transportation-related; short of tearing up highways and relocating airports, officials have no obvious solutions. And law enforcement agencies may not have the resources to patrol with decibel meters and seek out violators.

Several years ago, Boise State's Barber and a team of scientists installed 15 speakers in an Idaho woodland and played traffic noises to create a "phantom road" over half a mile of terrain. They found that 30% of songbirds moved elsewhere once the noise began, and many other species that remained struggled to gain weight.

In another experiment, Barber found that by asking visitors to voluntarily keep quiet at Muir Woods National Monument, a redwood forest near San Francisco, researchers measured an increase in birds near the trail.

Early efforts to regulate noise began in 1972, when the U.S. Environmental Protection Agency created the Office of Noise Abatement and Control, which set policy standards that many states used as benchmarks for their own regulations. Those included noise limits for the trucking industry, construction equipment and the transportation sector.

But when the Reagan administration shut down the office a decade later, citing a desire to transfer more regulatory power to local governments, states' appetite for noise policy withered as well, experts say. As a result, noise pollution has grown largely unchecked in prevalence and intensity.

The EPA argued that local communities could better regulate noise, said Les Blomberg, executive director of the Noise Pollution Clearinghouse, a nonprofit that tracks noise regulations throughout the country. "We've spent the last 40 years proving that wrong. Local communities can do a lot to regulate noise, but a lot of noise comes from noise sources in interstate commerce."

In 2017, the National Park Service found that human-caused sounds at least doubled natural noise levels in 63% of protected lands in the United States, such as parks and forests. The agency's Natural Sounds and Night Skies Division is behind one of the few federal efforts to deal with the noise issue. But with limited jurisdiction and regulatory power, it has mainly contributed research and small-scale changes such as using quieter tools and vehicles.

Washington's Quiet Sanctuaries

In 2005, acoustic ecologist Gordon Hempton dubbed a hidden spot in Olympic's Hoh Rainforest the One Square Inch of Silence, the quietest location in the contiguous United States. He's made it his mission to protect this place, and he's among many state residents concerned by the Navy's proposal to increase training flights of its Growler jets over the park.

"Prior to the Navy arriving, it was not only the least noise-polluted national park in the U.S., it was also the most noise-diverse," he said. "There are sounds you can't hear anywhere else."

One Square Inch is about a 3-mile hike into the rainforest, amid chest-high ferns and moss-covered trees. The nearby Hoh River babbles in the distance, while nearby birds chirp incessantly. At regular intervals, though—rarely longer than half an hour—the forest buzzes with the whine of a distant plane, or rumbles at a low-passing jet. According to Hempton, 80% of flights over the area are now conducted by the military.

"You add noise pollution into the background, and the owl that's hunting at night can no longer hear the soft scratching of the rodent underneath the leaves," Hempton said. "The consequences on wildlife are large enough that it is literally creating species shifts in natural areas."

The Navy's plan, which would increase by about a third its operations from a nearby air station, has prompted residents and organizations to form a coalition called the Sound Defense Alliance.

"We are squeezing all those natural sounds out of our environment," said Larry Morrell, the alliance's executive director. "We're trying to protect an extremely valuable and increasingly scarce natural resource, which is quiet. … Once you lose the quiet, it's really hard to get it back."

The Navy has said the training is vital, and it stands behind its environmental review of the proposal, which found that the expansion is not likely to "jeopardize the continued existence" of endangered species.

Michael Welding, a public affairs officer with Naval Air Station Whidbey Island, said in an email that the Navy could not comment on questions related to its endangered species analysis because of pending litigation.

However, he noted that the Navy already conducts an average of 2,300 Growler flights a year over the area that includes the park, and the proposal would only raise that by an additional 300 flights. Welding also said the Olympic Peninsula is an important training area, both because of its geographic diversity and airspace availability.

The attorney general's office did not respond to a request for comment.

On another front, the Port of Seattle also is trying to crack down on noise. It oversees the docking of massive container ships that cross the Pacific Ocean and are the loudest ships on the water.

Port of Seattle Commissioner Fred Felleman said the orcas are such a popular cause that many in the maritime industry might voluntarily slow vessel speeds and stay away from whale feeding areas, while bolstering research on the effects of underwater noise.

The port also has provided on-shore power sources for ships to plug into while they're docked, so they no longer have to run noisy generators while they're sitting in the water.

Scott Veirs, an oceanographer who runs Orcasound, a network of live hydrophones in Puget Sound, called ships the "biggest knob we can turn" to help orcas.

> **Most of the loudest sources are transportation-related, short of tearing up highways and relocating airports, officials have no obvious solutions.**

"Fifteen percent of ships are responsible for half of the radiated noise," he said. "If we replaced them with the best performers, we'd be well on our way to solving the problem. ... If we can reduce the noise from ships in the next 5 years, that's equivalent to getting [orcas] more access to the scarce salmon."

Regulators Face Hurdles

Michael Jasny, director of the Natural Resources Defense Council's Marine Mammal Protection Project, said few states are engaged with noise as an environmental issue. He noted a South Carolina state agency's recent move to block seismic surveys in state waters in the Atlantic Ocean, which blast the ocean floor with loud air guns to search for oil and gas. Many other coastal cities have bans on such surveys, but much more regulation is needed, he said.

"I don't think states have been terribly proactive—other than Washington state and South Carolina—in issuing their own laws," he said. "It's difficult to regulate outside of state waters. There's absolutely a role for states to play in some sectors, but ... there's a limit on the reach of states."

That's why noise pollution remains a thorny—and generally unaddressed—problem for states. Quiet advocates say it will take drastic measures just to prevent things from getting worse. Barber, the Boise State scientist, believes the country needs to stop building new roads and increase public transportation on existing corridors. But states have little say over the interstate highway system or federal airspace.

In Washington state, it remains unclear to what extent leaders will try to clamp down further on noise pollution. In response to Ferguson's legal challenge, the Navy has said it will re-evaluate whether its flight plans violate the Endangered Species Act, looking at disturbances to the marbled murrelet, a threatened seabird. That review is expected to be completed early next year.

While the bill Rolfes sponsored easily passed, requiring whale-watch tour boats to stay a greater distance from orcas and forcing all vessels to slow down when orcas are nearby, she said it's just the start.

"We did not address vessel noise in general and the impact of noise on the underwater environment," she said. "There's a lot of work to be done."

Further efforts to limit vessel noise around orcas could include everything from speed limits to different routes to quieter engines and propellers. How much of that would come from new laws as opposed to industry recommendations or incentives is another open question.

McCann, the ferry official working on the noise study, said awareness has been a critical first step in creating momentum.

"It's something that we're seeing industrywide, people taking it more seriously," he said. "The hope is that we're leading by example and providing a road map for other maritime partners."

Print Citations

CMS: Brown, Alex. "Noise Pollution Hurts Wildlife, but States Have Trouble Turning Down the Volume." In *The Reference Shelf: Pollution,* edited by Micah L. Issitt, 104-108. Amenia, NY: Grey House Publishing, 2020.

MLA: Brown, Alex. "Noise Pollution Hurts Wildlife, but States Have Trouble Turning Down the Volume." *The Reference Shelf: Pollution,* edited by Micah L. Issitt, Grey Housing Publishing, 2020, pp. 104-108.

APA: Brown, A. (2020). Noise pollution hurts wildlife, but states have trouble turning down the volume. In Micah L. Issitt (Ed.), *The reference shelf: Pollution* (pp. 104-108). Amenia, NY: Grey Housing Publishing.

Light Pollution Is a Big Problem, But You Can Help

By Joe Rao
Space.com, February 23, 2018

Back in the mid-'70s during the summertime, several astronomy-minded friends and I would pile into my beat-up Chevy Impala and travel a couple hundred miles north of New York City up Interstate 87 to Warrensburg, New York. Not far from there was a campsite where we would spend time with our telescopes, observing the dark, star-spangled skies of the Adirondacks. Of course, other campers always gravitated to our campsite, where we enjoyed pointing out celestial sights and providing star-identification tips.

On one of those nights, a young woman asked me what was that "long cloud" that appeared to stretch across the sky each night from horizon to horizon. That "long cloud" was, of course, the Milky Way, which, under those very dark skies, appeared so bright that it actually cast a dim shadow. I asked her how it was that she didn't know its identity. She responded that this was her very first time away from home and that she had never camped outside before.

"Where is home?" I asked.

"Brooklyn" was her response. Hardly a place where one can see a dark, starry sky!

A sad commentary, perhaps, on one way that "progress" is stymieing our appreciation of nature. Indeed, no longer can residents in most metropolitan areas or even their nearby suburbs be treated to a view of our home galaxy, the Milky Way. And that's not the only celestial sight that is no longer available.

Back in 1996 and again in 1997, skywatchers around the world were treated to the sight of two magnificent naked-eye comets: Hyakutake and Hale-Bopp. From dark skies, both were accompanied by beautifully long, gossamer tails, but from urban areas, they appeared as little more than bright fuzz balls.

A side note here: I grew up in the Throgs Neck section of the Bronx, and during the 1960s, I could see quite a bit of the night sky from my backyard. But today, the city has gotten brighter. Much brighter. So bright, in fact, that now I can easily read a newspaper at night near my childhood stomping grounds without a flashlight. And the skies at my old Adirondack campsite have gotten noticeably brighter, too. What was once a sea of stars against a pitch-black background now looks more like a shade of charcoal gray.

Judging by the number of visible stars, my observations show that light pollution has made the night sky over Warrensburg, New York, about four times brighter since the mid-'70s. And at various points along the horizon, there are now small domes of light indicating the presence of nearby towns, the brightest of which is Lake George, a popular tourist center several miles to the south.

All of this can be traced to one thing: the curse of light pollution.

Disastrous Practical Effects

Light pollution is the excessive or misdirected outdoor lighting that is threatening to destroy virtually all casual stargazing. Throughout much of the United States, for instance, millions upon millions of precious watts are wasted because poorly designed streetlamps send a portion of their light into the sky. But it's not just stargazers who need to be concerned. While some may scoff at preserving the beauty of the night sky, there are other facets of light pollution that have a direct impact on all of us. Here are just a few examples:

Energy consumption: Joshua Filmer of Futurism.com reported in 2013 that at least 30 percent of street lighting is wasted—light that shines up into the sky, where it does no good. "Calculations show that 22,000 gigawatt-hours a year are wasted. At $0.10 per kilowatt-hour, the cost of that wasted energy is $2.2 billion a year," Filmer wrote. "That's 3.6 tons of coal or 12.9 million barrels of oil wasted every year to produce this lost light."

Wildlife: John Metcalfe at Citylab.com reported last year that lights are disorienting birds, with deadly results. "Many species migrate by night and are perilously dazzled by artificial illumination, for reasons we don't yet completely understand," Metcalfe wrote. "Lights on skyscrapers, airports, and stadiums draw birds into urban areas, where they smack into walls and windows or each other, or flap around and eventually perish from exhaustion-related complications."

Human health: According to an article published in the journal *Environmental Health Perspectives*, several studies over the past two decades have suggested that the modern practice of keeping our bodies exposed to artificial light at night increases cancer risk, especially for cancers that require hormones to grow, such as breast and prostate cancers.

LEDs: Good ... and Bad

Regarding energy consumption, the past five or six years have seen a slow transformation from garish, peach-colored, high-pressure sodium vapor streetlights—which have long been recognized to be energy-inefficient—to light-emitting diode (LED) streetlights, which use solid-state technology to convert electricity into light.

In contrast to old-fashioned incandescent light bulbs used in sodium vapor streetlights, LEDs do not possess filaments that burn out, nor do they get very warm. Because of their improved quality and lower cost, LEDs are now gradually replacing conventional streetlights for outdoor lighting in communities around the world. Good news, right?

Well, not necessarily.

Unfortunately, white LED lighting also tends to transmit high levels of blue light, which can pose potential health hazards.

> **Light pollution is the excessive or misdirected outdoor lighting that is threatening to destroy virtually all casual stargazing.**

According to the International Dark-Sky Association (IDA), "Outdoor lighting with high blue light content is more likely to contribute to light pollution because it has a significantly larger geographic reach than lighting with less blue light. Blue-rich white light sources are also known to increase glare and compromise human vision. And in natural settings, blue light at night has been shown to adversely affect wildlife behavior and reproduction."

Ways to correct this problem include the following:

1. Properly using shields to direct the light downward, where it is needed.
2. Converting to "warm white" LEDs, which minimize blue emissions.
3. Using adapters that can dim lamps during the late-night and predawn hours.
4. Avoiding the temptation to use extra lights because LEDs are more energy-efficient and thus ultimately less expensive over time.

That last suggestion seems to be of especially increasing concern. As an artifact of the lower costs of LEDs, many people are now unnecessarily illuminating places that they didn't bother to light before, like the outsides of buildings and other infrastructure, according to a study in the journal *Science Advances*.

What Can You Do?

The IDA, founded 30 years ago, gathers and disseminates light-pollution information and solutions. It has played a pivotal role in turning the tide in the light-pollution war. The IDA is winning over key sectors of the nonastronomical public—including government groups, sections of the lighting industry and electric utilities—arguing that good lighting for astronomers equals energy savings and more attractive surroundings for everyone else.

For more information on how to get involved, you can contact the IDA directly. (And to learn more about light pollution, you can also watch "Losing the Dark," a short planetarium show and video on light pollution produced by the IDA.)

You can also join thousands of other students, families, educators and citizen scientists by participating in an international event called "Globe at Night." This event, which is free to attend, is designed to observe and record how constellations appear from different locations, as a means of measuring the brightness of the sky at a variety of urban and rural sites.

Prospective observers can report their results online by comparing the number of stars seen in the night sky with a set of template images that depict the stars' visibility in varying levels of light pollution. Participation is open to anyone, anywhere in the world, who can get outside and look skyward.

Not convinced that extra lighting is a problem? Check out these nighttime satellite views of Earth, courtesy of NASA's Suomi NPP satellite. Additional images from Suomi NPP taken between 2010 and 2016 clearly show how light pollution is on the rise around the globe.

Lastly, you can do your part by learning more about light pollution and by taking steps to reduce extra nighttime lighting in your own town and backyard. In addition to letting you see the stars better, these steps may also save you money on electricity and help reduce the world's energy usage. Cities and towns that routinely put up ever-brighter lights for no reason other than "that's what we've always done" may think twice about spending the money if they hear just a few voices of opposition.

What are your town's lighting plans? Call your city or town hall today!

Remember, the night sky you save might be your own.

Print Citations

CMS: Rao, Joe. "Light Pollution Is a Big Problem, but You Can Help." In *The Reference Shelf: Pollution,* edited by Micah L. Issitt, 109-112. Amenia, NY: Grey House Publishing, 2020.

MLA: Rao, Joe. "Light Pollution Is a Big Problem, but You Can Help." *The Reference Shelf: Pollution,* edited by Micah L. Issitt, Grey Housing Publishing, 2020, pp. 109-112.

APA: Rao, J. (2020). Light pollution is a big problem, but you can help. In Micah L. Issitt (Ed.), *The reference shelf: Pollution* (pp. 109-112). Amenia, NY: Grey Housing Publishing.

The Vanishing Night: Light Pollution Threatens Ecosystems

By Diana Kwon
The Scientist, September 30, 2018

As darkness fell over Manhattan on the ninth anniversary of the September 11 attack, two beams were shot into the sky at the site where the Twin Towers once stood. The commemorative lights had appeared annually since the towers fell, but in 2010 onlookers noticed something unusual: countless white sparkles glittering within the white beams.

The mysterious white objects turned out to be thousands of migrating birds. Although the public had just taken notice of this spectacle, conservationists had been aware of the phenomenon for several years. Shortly after the tribute first appeared, New York City Audubon, a conservation group, helped initiate a program to monitor the installation and temporarily shut off the lights whenever too many birds got caught in the beams. In a later analysis of the bird populations on memorial nights between 2008 and 2016, researchers found that, although the short-term shutdowns were effective, approximately 1 million animals had been attracted to the glowing memorial and had become distracted from their normal migratory routes.[1]

This annual demonstration of how artificial illumination can influence animal behavior is but one instance of a much bigger problem. Around 80 percent of all humans—and more than 99 percent of people in the US and Europe—now live under light-polluted skies. In addition to direct lighting from urban infrastructure, light reflected from clouds and aerosols, known as skyglow, is brightening nights even in unlit habitats. As electric lights become more energy- and cost-efficient, the proportion of lit surfaces keeps rising. Meanwhile, the list of organisms that researchers document to be affected by Earth's unnatural glow is growing right along with it.

In 2002, the University of Southern California geographer Travis Longcore, also science director of the Los Angeles–based nonprofit the Urban Wildlands Group, and colleagues organized the first North American conference on the ecological consequences of light pollution. This inspired a growing interest in the scientific community that eventually led to a handful of large-scale projects that launched in Europe around 2010, says Thomas Davies, a postdoctoral ecologist at Bangor University in the UK. "That's when we started to see this exponential growth in the research output in this field."

Over the last 16 years, researchers have uncovered the many nuanced ways that light can affect individual species and have started to build a bigger picture of the effects on ecosystems. "It's become clear that light pollution is a major anthropogenic pressure on the environment," says Kevin Gaston, an ecologist at the University of Exeter in the UK.

And it's a uniquely disruptive pressure in that life on Earth evolved to the beat of the circadian cycle, and bright, constant light at night is a very recent phenomenon in evolutionary time, adds Therésa Jones, a behavioral ecologist at the University of Melbourne in Australia. "We have nothing in our genetic make-up that has been exposed to this type of challenge. It's completely unprecedented in the history of the Earth."

Fatal Attraction

In the 1880s, Swedish-American ornithologist Ludwig Kumlien noted that a 200-foot-tall, illuminated observation tower in Milwaukee, Wisconsin, was attracting migrating birds in the evening—and that many perished after colliding with the lights or the surrounding electric wires.[2] This was one of the earliest reports of what is now a well-known effect of artificial nighttime lighting: its ability to draw in wildlife.

Since then, researchers have identified several other animals that succumb to light's fatal allure. Insects are perhaps the most obvious example—many of these critters are nocturnal, and a wide variety of species, including beetles, mayflies, and moths, will cluster around streetlamps, floodlights, and other sources of nighttime illumination. Although the factors underlying this so-called "flight-to-light" behavior remain unclear, the consequences are well documented: increased rates of injury, exhaustion, and predation.

Evening lighting can also fragment animals' habitats, as strings of lamps limit the movement of organisms from one place to another. In one field experiment, Franz Hölker, a freshwater ecologist at the Berlin-based Leibniz-Institute of Freshwater Ecology and Inland Fisheries, and his colleagues discovered that street lights could draw in moths passing within a radius of approximately 23 meters.[3] Given that lampposts—at least in Europe—are typically around 20 to 45 meters apart, Hölker explains, the area from which they draw in insects often overlaps, creating a magnet that traps the animals and reduces their ability to disperse through the environment.

Certain organisms may adapt to light over time, potentially limiting the negative effects of the exposure. In 2016, a pair of Swiss researchers discovered that adult ermine moths (*Yponomeuta cagnagella*) from bright urban areas were less likely to be attracted to lights than their counterparts from dark, rural regions.[4] This is likely a "genuine adaptation," Gaston says. "The selection pressure to not fly to light is quite high if you are constantly exposed to it, and you're suffering high mortality or energetic costs."

But so far, the ermine moths are the only documented example of such an adaptation to avoid artificial light. Whether the behavior of other animal populations will change in this way remains an open question, says Gaston. In addition, as light levels are one of many characteristics that differ between urban and rural areas, it is difficult for scientists to rule out the contributions of noise, air pollution, and other environmental stressors present in developed regions of the world.

Out of Sync

Most organisms, from bacteria to people, have biological rhythms that help keep them aligned with the day-night cycles that occur as the planet rotates about its axis. These cadences are entrained by a variety of external signals, with light as the most important cue. As darkness disappears, that regulation can go awry.

Artificially extended days can modify the timing of tightly controlled daily activities, such as foraging and sleep.[5] Some diurnal species, such as the great tit (*Parus major*), may continue searching for food later in the day, while nocturnal organisms—certain mice or bats, for example—spend less time out hunting or foraging.

Light pollution can also distort seasonal and lunar rhythms, which are responsible for biological events such as reproduction and migration. Davide Dominoni, a postdoctoral ecologist at the Netherlands Institute of Ecology in Wageningen, and colleagues have found that constant, low levels of illumination at night (0.3 lux, 20 times lower than the intensity of the average street lamp in Munich, Germany, where the study took place) caused European blackbirds, *Turdus merula*, to develop their reproductive systems a month earlier than counterparts reared with dark nights.[6] Other researchers have found that light pollution can delay birth in wallabies,[7] advance egg laying in songbirds,[8] and alter the migration patterns of salmon.[9]

Such perturbations may be mediated by changes in levels of melatonin, a hormone that is produced primarily at night and plays a key role in light's effect on circadian cycles. The secretion of this chemical is known to be suppressed by blue light, which is present in high amounts in electronic devices and light-emitting diodes (LEDs), a type of lighting gaining popularity for use in street lamps thanks to its low cost and high energy efficiency. Reduced levels of melatonin have been measured in humans exposed to blue light.[10] Last year, a group led by researchers at the University of Haifa in Israel found that people exposed to computer screens at night experienced modified circadian oscillations—specifically, lower nighttime melatonin production and a smaller nocturnal drop in body temperature—as well as altered sleep patterns.[11]

> **Artificially extended days can modify the timing of tightly controlled daily activities, such as foraging and sleep.**

Experiments in the lab have shown that exposure to light at night can also dampen melatonin secretion in a variety of other animal species, including birds, fish, and insects. Jones and her team, for example, found that crickets reared under constant light had lower melatonin levels and impairments in immune function compared with those exposed to 12 hours of illumination per day.[12]

Despite the growing evidence that nighttime glow can alter daily and seasonal cycles, scientists currently have "very little evidence for strong effects, at least in vertebrates, on the fitness of animals," Dominoni says. "I'm interested in trying to figure out whether the effects of light pollution on circadian and seasonal rhythms . . . have long-term consequences on the health of these animals."

For some species, the potential harm of light pollution may be offset by benefits. In recent work published as a preprint earlier this year, Jones and colleagues found that Australian garden orb-weaving spiders (*Eriophora biapicata*) exposed to artificial light at night end up maturing faster and with fewer molts, being smaller as adults, and laying fewer eggs.[13] Outside the lab, however, the researchers observed a compensating advantage: spiders living near streetlights ate more than individuals living in darker locales, due to the abundance of potential prey congregating around the lights (unpublished). "Physiologically they were being affected, but ultimately they were doing okay because they gained this benefit from the change in the predator-prey relationship," Jones says.

Chain Reactions

During the summers of 2014 and 2015, Eva Knop, a community ecologist at the University of Bern in Switzerland, and her team spent several nights wandering through meadows wearing night-vision goggles, in search of nocturnal pollinators. The researchers had positioned street lamps over seven cabbage thistle (*Cirsium oleraceum*) patches in remote meadows in the foothills of the Swiss Alps previously unexposed to nighttime illumination. They then compared insects on the plants in the lit areas to those on plants in nearby, unlit control regions.

This investigation revealed a 62 percent reduction in nocturnal visits to the cabbage thistles in light-polluted areas, which led to a corresponding 13 percent drop in fruit production among the illuminated plants.[14] This decreased output could cause a decline in diurnal pollinator populations, which rely on the plants as a key source of food, the study authors suggest. "We need further experimental work to prove these indirect effects, but this shows that the negative effect at night could indirectly propagate into the day," Knop says.

A number of recent experiments in Europe have started to reveal how light pollution influences species interactions. At the University of Exeter, Gaston and his colleagues have set up grassland mesocosms, mini ecosystems within wooden cubes, each containing various plant, herbivore, and carnivore species. By exposing the enclosures to LEDs of varying intensities—low levels to mimic skyglow, medium levels corresponding to streetlamps, and high levels akin to stadium lighting—Gaston's team has found that light pollution can have profound effects on predator-prey interactions.[15]

In one experiment, for example, the team found that in 48 mesocosms that were exposed to low-intensity light for a few months, aphid populations shrank by approximately 50 percent due to increased predation by parasitoid wasps. Conversely, predators spent less time on the prey's host plants lit by more intense lights, leading to fewer aphid deaths. "Because of the interactions [between species], you might actually see quite severe effects even at quite low light levels," Gaston says. "It's not just how you respond, it's what your natural enemies and competitors are doing."

Such ecosystem-level effects of light pollution can influence population dynamics and even community productivity. At the Westhavelland Nature Park, one of the darkest regions in Germany, Hölker and his colleagues compared microbial communities in freshwater sediments from two sites in a shallow agricultural drainage ditch—one site lit by artificial light at night and the other left dark. After five months, they found a significant increase in photosynthesizing microbes, suggesting that these organisms were using nighttime lighting as an energy source.[16] Subsequent laboratory experiments revealed that exposing sediments to artificial light also perturbed the seasonal changes that typically occur in the microbial population. Without exposure to light pollution, there were clear winter and summer communities of bacteria and algae, Hölker says. "[But] after one year of illumination, this difference was no longer significant—the temporal structure was lost."

This change in the composition of microbial communities corresponded with a shift in the ecosystem's productivity. Under artificial lights, the microorganisms produced less carbon dioxide than those unexposed to evening illumination, likely a consequence of nighttime photosynthesis. In the long term, the researchers suggest, this could reduce the amount of carbon released from these freshwater systems into the biosphere over time.

"We naturally tend to think about the impacts [of light pollution] on individual species in isolation," says Gaston. "But I think what's becoming apparent now is that those networks of interactions are really vital to understanding the consequences of light at night."

Shrinking Numbers

Last year, researchers reported that flying-insect populations in Germany had dropped by more than 75 percent over the past three decades.[17] This dramatic loss in invertebrate life made headlines, and a coauthor of the study warned that such declines have set the Earth on course for an "ecological Armageddon." Of course, the question on everyone's mind was: What's the cause? "When this study came out, they were thinking about land-use change, climate change, and pesticides," Hölker says. But these factors alone could not explain the population plunge. Light pollution might be the missing piece of the puzzle, adds Hölker, whose team recently discovered that the decimated regions also had high levels of evening illumination.[18]

Light pollution could dramatically alter populations of vertebrates as well. Field experiments by Kamiel Spoelstra, a biologist at the Netherlands Institute of Ecology, and colleagues have revealed that fast-flying Pipistrellus bats accumulate under certain colors of light that slow-flying *Myotis* and *Plecotus* bats avoid.[19] The slow bats may be light-shy because exposing themselves under light could make them more vulnerable to predators, whereas agile bats may be able to enjoy the feast of insects that accumulate under the lights, Spoelstra explains.

Over time, it is possible that "if you have many lights outside, these light-shy bats simply lose habitats," Spoelstra says. "It may be that the more lighting we have, the more common the common species and the rarer the less-common species become."

But examining the effects of artificial light on animal populations is difficult, and strong evidence of light pollution's long-term repercussions remains scarce. To appreciate the true scale of light pollution's effects, the best place to look would be in regions that have only recently been exposed to nighttime lights. A recent analysis found that between 2012 and 2016, the artificially lit outdoor surface area of the earth increased at an estimated rate of 2.2 percent per year, with much of the growth occurring in South America, Africa, and Asia.[20] This expansion has largely been facilitated by energy-efficient LEDs, Davies says. "So you get remote lights that are being put up in parts of the world that have previously been dark for the whole of evolutionary time."

As scientists uncover more and more evidence of the harms of nighttime light, they are beginning to work with designers, architects, and government officials to protect the planet's wildlife. Spoelstra, for example, has worked with Dutch policy makers to illuminate some areas with red light instead of white to prevent disruption to bat populations. However, this problem "can't be solved by changing the spectrum alone," Spoelstra says. Other modifications, such as limiting the times when roads are illuminated, putting motion sensors on lights, and shielding lamps so light does not spill into the sky or adjacent forests, are also necessary, he adds.

By themselves, these solutions are not enough to fight the effects of the increasingly luminous nights across the globe. Animals will not be able to evolve fast enough to adapt to the changes humans make on the planet, Longcore says. "We need to make either individual or collective decisions to not make the world even more light polluted than it already is."

Evening Hues

Artificial lights come in a range of colors. Low-pressure sodium lamps, which are typically used to brighten streets at night, have a distinct yellow hue. Light-emitting diodes (LEDs), on the other hand, offer illumination that is more energy-efficient, but the commonly used white LEDs typically produce large amounts of blue light. Scientists have long suspected that blue-rich lighting is the most harmful to wildlife. Decades of research have revealed that the cool hue is attractive to many animals—particularly insects—and can suppress the production of melatonin, a crucial hormone for regulating circadian rhythms.

In a recent analysis, University of Southern California geographer Travis Longcore and colleagues compiled previously published data on organisms' responses to light across the spectrum to calculate the predicted effects of different lighting types. This work demonstrated that blue-rich lights indeed pose the greatest risk for the well-being of a wide variety of species, including insects, birds, and fish (*J Exp Zool*, doi:10.1002/jez.2184, 2018).

Now, conservationists are looking to capitalize on this information to protect wildlife. In Florida, for instance, the Fish and Wildlife Conservation Commission now recommends the use of red or amber LEDs to avoid attracting hatchling sea turtles. Similarly, some areas in the Netherlands have installed red lights to make their evening skies safer for bats.

But even these colors can have adverse effects. For example, red lights tend to attract migrating birds—a problem recently recognized by the US Federal Aviation Administration, which announced in 2015 that it would require communication tower operators to replace steady red lights with flashing ones to reduce their allure.

References

1. B.M. Van Doren et al., "High-intensity urban light installation dramatically alters nocturnal bird migration," *PNAS*, 114:11175–80, 2017.
2. L. Kumlien, "Observations on bird migration at Milwaukee," *The Auk*, 5:325–28, 1888.
3. T. Degen et al., "Street lighting: Sex-independent impacts on moth movement," *J Anim Ecol*, 85:1352–60, 2016.
4. F. Altermatt, D. Ebert, "Reduced flight-to-light behaviour of moth populations exposed to long-term urban light pollution," *Bio Lett*, 12:20160111, 2016.
5. K.J. Gaston et al., "Impacts of artificial light at night on biological timings," *Annu Rev Ecol Evol Syst*, 48:49–68, 2017.
6. D. Dominoni et al., "Artificial light at night advances avian reproductive physiology," *Proc R Soc B*, 280:20123017, 2013.
7. K.A. Robert et al., "Artificial light at night desynchronizes strictly seasonal reproduction in a wild mammal," *Proc R Soc B*, 282:20151745, 2015.
8. B. Kempenaers et al., "Artificial night lighting affects dawn song, extra-pair siring success, and lay date in songbirds," *Curr Biol*, 20:1735–39, 2010.
9. W.D. Riley et al., "Street lighting disrupts the diel migratory pattern of wild Atlantic salmon, Salmo salar L., smolts leaving their natal stream," *Aquaculture*, 330–333:74–81, 2012.
10. K.E. West et al., "Blue light from light-emitting diodes elicits a dose-dependent suppression of melatonin in humans," *J Appl Physiol*, 110:619–26, 2011.
11. Green et al., "Evening light exposure to computer screens disrupts human sleep, biological rhythms, and attention abilities," *Chronobiol Int*, 34:855–65, 2017.
12. J. Durrant et al., "Constant illumination reduces circulating melatonin and impairs immune function in the cricket Teleogryllus commodus," *PeerJ*, 3:e1075, 2015.
13. N.J. Willmott et al., "Artificial light at night alters life history in a nocturnal orb-web spider," *PeerJ Preprints*, 6:e26943v1, 2018.
14. E. Knop et al., "Artificial light at night as a new threat to pollination," *Nature*, 548:206–09, 2017.

15. D. Sanders et al., "Low levels of artificial light at night change food web dynamics." *Curr Biol,* 28:2474–78, 2018.

16. F. Hölker et al., "Microbial diversity and community respiration in freshwater sediments influenced by artificial light at night," *Philos Trans R Soc Lond B Biol Sci,* 370:20140130, 2015.

17. C.A. Hallman et al., "More than 75 percent decline in 27 years in total flying insect biomass in protected areas," *PLOS One,* 12:e0185809, 2017.

18. M. Grubsic et al., "Insect declines and agroecosystems: does light pollution matter?" *Ann Appl Biol,* 173: 180-9, 2018.

19. K. Spoelstra et al., "Response of bats to light with different spectra: Light-shy and agile bat presence is affected by white and green, but not red light," *Proc R Soc B,* 284:20170075, 2017.

20. C.C.M. Kyba et al., "Artificially lit surface of Earth at night increasing in radiance and extent," *Sci Adv,* 3:e1701528, 2017.

Print Citations

CMS: Kwon, Diana. "The Vanishing Night: Light Pollution Threatens Ecosystems." In *The Reference Shelf: Pollution,* edited by Micah L. Issitt, 113-120. Amenia, NY: Grey House Publishing, 2020.

MLA: Kwon, Diana. "The Vanishing Night: Light Pollution Threatens Ecosystems." *The Reference Shelf: Pollution,* edited by Micah L. Issitt, Grey Housing Publishing, 2020, pp. 113-120.

APA: Kwon, D. (2020). The vanishing night: Light pollution threatens ecosystems. In Micah L. Issitt (Ed.), *The reference shelf: Pollution* (pp. 113-120). Amenia, NY: Grey Housing Publishing.

Where Light Pollution Is Seeping into the Rural Night Sky

By Linda Poon
Bloomberg CityLab, February 11, 2020

The rule of thumb is that if you want to see the Milky Way, you have to venture out to the countryside. That's where the illumination from streetlights and brightly lit offices that floods cities hasn't obscured the night sky. But a recent map tracking the artificial lighting seen at night through satellite imagery paints a very different picture. In the map of the United States by Tim Wallace, a cartographer at Descartes Labs, metropolitan areas like New York City, Los Angeles, and Chicago are dark, while rural areas in the Dakotas and sparsely populated towns right outside major urban centers stand out as bright spots.

It's not that cities have dramatically reduced light pollution (they haven't). "Most of the light is coming from places where there are lots of people," Wallace says of traditional nighttime maps, which look almost identical to population density maps. Instead, Wallace's map is the result of taking 2015 nighttime data from the National Oceanic and Atmospheric Administration and (roughly) normalizing it for population so that it shows the amount of light emitted per person in an area.

What's left is a cartographic look at a problem that's often overshadowed: Light pollution is also a threat to rural areas, and it's disrupting ecosystems that rely on natural darkness. Not only does rural lighting make star-gazing harder for enthusiasts and space researchers, it also seeps into nearby habitats, changing the resting and feeding behavior of wildlife. For nocturnal migratory birds, for example, these sources of illumination can be confusing, and even deadly. It's a problem that the International Dark-Sky Association has been calling attention to.

"We've always had this two-pronged approach: addressing the problem largely where it exists, which is in the cities, while recognizing the rural areas where darkness still exists [as] a form of natural resource," says John Barentine, the organization's policy director. "So we are concerned about some of these places that are lighting on Tim's map."

Where is the light coming from? Aside from Disney World in Florida, and airports, Wallace and Barentine point to three particular kinds of economic activities in rural areas: oil and gas extraction, the expansion of warehouse hubs, and increasingly, greenhouses.

Looking at Wallace's map, it's hard to miss the burst of light in western North Dakota. That's the location of the Bakken Shale, one of the U.S.'s largest oil producers. Production peaked in spring

> **Not only does rural lighting make stargazing harder for enthusiasts and space researchers, it also seeps into nearby habitats, changing the resting and feeding behavior of wildlife.**

2015 at 1.33 million barrels a day. Barentine points to two other spots that light up for the same reason: the Eagle Ford Shale in South Texas, and the Permian Basin, located in western Texas and southeastern New Mexico. The pollution comes from a mix of on-site lighting for worker safety and the flaring of excess natural gas.

"If you draw a box around the bright blob in western North Dakota and add up all that light, there's approximately as much light being emitted by that operation as there is by the incorporated boundaries of Chicago," he says. That's not unique to that the Bakken Shale. A 2018 investigation from *The Revelator* found that, based on 2013 data from NOAA, the brightest sections of the Eagle Ford Shale are as bright as Reno, Nevada.

Between 2010 and 2013, when the U.S. was in the midst of a significant oil boom, measurements from the National Park Service's Natural Sounds and Night Skies Division found that man-made light visible in the north unit of Theodore Roosevelt National Park, near the Bakken oilfield, increased by 500 percent—faster than at any other national park in the country, according to *Inside Energy*. The University of Texas's McDonald Observatory, which is a member of the International Dark-Sky Association, has been working with oil companies to find ways to mitigate light pollution. In 2018, the observatory laid out a set of guidelines for improving lighting practices at rig sites. It recommended readjusting lighting fixtures at sites so they don't point up at the sky and redesigning blueprints to minimize the amount of lighting needed.

The Expansion of Warehouse Hubs

While much of downtown Chicago is blacked out on Wallace's map, the town of Joliet just southeast of it shines brightly. Similarly in California, Los Angeles remains dim but the cities that sit on the edge—Riverside and San Bernardino—stand out in stark contrast.

These three areas are just a handful of the places that have become dominated by warehouses, data centers, and fulfillment and distribution hubs. As e-commerce took off over the last decade, once-cheap farmland became a popular site for tech and retail companies. "One of the things we kept seeing over and over again were these these little exurbs that 10 years ago might have had one DHL [warehouse], but now they have an Amazon fulfillment center and a DHL and something for Target," says Wallace, who worked with the *New York Times* last year tracking the transformation of America's landscape.

The real estate firm Cushman & Wakefield calculated that developers added nearly 850 million square feet of warehouse space between 2013 and 2017, more than double the amount built over the previous five years. And the buildings keep getting bigger. Amazon alone, for example, has nearly 350 facilities across the U.S.; several are more than 1 million square feet. "These buildings are massive," says Wallace, "and they pop in this light map because the parking lots are lit up and the buildings often have lights on [at night] as well."

According to Barentine, the rise of these industrial hubs aligns with the rise in sales of exterior lighting fixtures, which have seen some of the most dramatic spikes in popularity in recent years.

Greenhouse and Cannabis Industry

When asked if any places stood out to him, Wallace pointed to Madison, Maine. There, surrounded by acres of empty fields and forest, is a 42-acre indoor farm— about the size of 32 football fields—operated by the tomato grower Backyard Farms. On Wallace's map, the farm is one of two spots that glows prominently. "That blew my mind. You can see this tomato greenhouse in this super-remote area in Maine," he says. "It's a massive complex where their lights must be on at night."

As it turns out, the legal cannabis and horticulture industries are on the Dark-Sky Association's radar as light pollution sources, and not just in rural areas, says Barentine. "Greenhouses are now built increasingly in suburban and even urban areas. [Companies] run those operations 24 hours a day, and for some good part of the night, they're running lighting at full blast." It's not just the duration of the light that concerns conservationists, he adds, but new LED technology that allows growers to change the color of the light to what their specific crops need.

Anecdotally, they've become a nuisance to nearby residents. In Snowflake, Arizona, last month, residents complained of a mysterious purple glow. The source? A 1.7 million-square-foot (40-acre) marijuana farm just a few miles away.

Early research also suggests that the unnaturally colored lighting can disrupt the plant cycle in wildlife corridors, which in turn, could affect the food supply. Barentine acknowledges that more research on the impact of greenhouse lighting is needed, but says the lack of regulation is a concern. "In isolation, light may not be a really serious hazard to species," he says. "But if they are already being stressed for other reasons, and you add that on top, it can be very significant."

Print Citations

CMS: Poon, Linda. "Where Light Is Seeping into the Rural Night Sky." In *The Reference Shelf: Pollution,* edited by Micah L. Issitt, 121-124. Amenia, NY: Grey House Publishing, 2020.

MLA: Poon, Linda. "Where Light Is Seeping into the Rural Night Sky." *The Reference Shelf: Pollution,* edited by Micah L. Issitt, Grey Housing Publishing, 2020, pp. 121-124.

APA: Poon, L. (2020). Where light is seeping into the rural night sky. In Micah L. Issitt (Ed.), *The reference shelf: Pollution* (pp. 121-124). Amenia, NY: Grey Housing Publishing.

5
Looking Ahead

An NOAA marine debris removal operation in 2014

Finding Solutions

Combating pollution is a worthy goal, as a world without pollution would be one in which humans and other creatures could live healthier lives. But much of the pollution created by humanity is a direct result of the technological innovations that have allowed them to advance and so combating pollution conflicts with other priorities. Pollution is a major, worldwide problem, and mainstream, familiar solutions are largely insufficient. The world may need to rely on innovators to lead the way. In 2020, a host of engineers and environmental scientists around the world are in the process of developing new strategies and technologies to address pollution issues, ranging from legislative to the cutting edge of digital technology.

Changing Cities

Air, noise, and light pollution are more severe in and around cities. The high density of both people and pollution-creating cars and household heating-cooling systems creates dense pockets of pollution that have made urban landscapes toxic. Some cities, like Los Angeles, New York, Milan, and Tokyo have dramatic levels of pollution that have proven difficult to combat because of population density. Because pollution is more severe in urban environments, many of the most innovative approaches to combating it involve ways to create "greener" cities. Solutions run the gamut, from small-scale innovations to major engineering projects designed to take a major bite out of pollution.

One of the ways that greener cities can be created is by enhancing plant life within urban areas. Plants can absorb and metabolize pollutants from the air and water and purify the air and water that returns to the Earth. However, demand for residential and commercial spaces eliminates green zones for trees and plants. Engineers and urban planners are attempting to make cities greener by creating better opportunities for plants to live and grow in urban environments. For instance, in Europe an innovative solution called "CityTree" benches demonstrates that a relatively small area can be redesigned to have a major impact on pollution. CityTree benches feature artfully designed pedestrian seating areas attached to large vertical planters containing thousands of tiny moss plants. The planters feature technology to capture and distribute rainwater, thereby making maintenance easier, and the mosses are planted in a dense medium rich in bacteria that will allow the moss and bacteria to absorb and purify the air and water that passes through the bench. The designers say that one of their benches purifies as much air as 275 trees, meaning that a relatively small number of benches distributed around a city could provide the pollution-modifying power of a small forest.[1]

The idea of creating vertical plantings can also be taken to the extreme, as represented by innovative "vertical forest" buildings that have been erected both in China and in Italy. Stefano Boeri's vertical forest tower in Milan, the "Bosco Verticale," was built in 2014 and features 900 trees, 5,000 shrubs, and 11,000 other plants arranged on planting platforms that cover the outer surface of a massive multistory apartment building. Boeri was then hired to create a massive version of his project, billed as a "forest city," in Liuzhou, China. This new city, composed primarily of vertical forest-type buildings, is intended to house more than 30,000 people and enough trees and plants to absorb more than 10,000 tons of CO_2 and 57 tons of other pollutants each year.

While green spaces and plantings might be the most natural way to address pollution, there are other ways to remove pollutants from air and water using engineering and chemical solutions. For instance, in 2015 engineers unveiled a new building in Milan, the 13,000-square-meter Palazzo Italia, designed to be one of the world's most ecofriendly buildings. The 9,000-square-meter façade is constructed of 900 biodynamic concrete panels containing titanium dioxide. When these panels come into contact with sunlight, the material absorbs air pollutants and transforms them into inert salts. The designers estimate that one building would remove the carbon pollution released by more than 1,000 cars each day. A similar structure, though with a different aesthetic design, is the Manuel Gea González Hospital in Mexico City, which is covered by 2,500 square meters of titanium dioxide capturing material.[2]

The discovery that titanium dioxide—a naturally occurring oxide version of titanium frequently used as a pigment—is effective in capturing and neutralizing pollution has also led to smaller-scale efforts. In the UK designer Helen Storey and chemist Tony Ryan have been working on a program for using titanium dioxide to create a detergent that will release a small amount of titanium oxide after laundering to attract and capture pollutants and then wash away at the next washing. Speaking to *Scientific American*, Storey stated her belief that addressing climate change required making everyday objects and practices "smarter," and claimed that their "smart" clothing design transforms the function of a common, everyday object.[3]

Liquid Courage

The other major forefront in the fight against pollution is the effort to protect oceans and rivers from the impact of human activity. Here, too, innovations from the realm of technology have emerged to preserve remaining sources of water. At one end of the spectrum, the problem of oceanic pollution has inspired massive public-private ventures to simply clean oceanic waters. The best-known program in this vein is the Ocean Cleanup," a program initiated in 2015 by 21-year-old Dutch environmental activist Boyan Slat, which is specifically focused on cleaning up plastic and other debris in the Great Pacific Garbage Patch. Over the years, the Ocean Cleanup project has evolved to become the largest pollution remediation program in the world. It has also expanded to set ships called "interceptors" into river systems to intercept plastic and other debris before it reaches the ocean. However, in 2019 Ocean Cleanup's most important garbage collecting device broke, as many experts had feared, revealing problems that plagued the program from the beginning. Writing in

The Verge in 2019, journalist Rachel Becker argues that the problem with the ocean cleanup is that it does not address the creation of pollution and cannot be a long-term sustainable solution.[4]

Another way in which water pollution might be addressed is by creating new methods for water treatment and processing. One example can be found in the company Anammox, created by Dutch scientist Mark van Loosdrecht, for which he won the 2012 Lee Kuan Yew Water Prize. Loosdrecht's program utilizes specially formulated strains of bacteria to remove pollution from water while utilizing far less energy, oxygen, and chemicals than other common forms of water treatment. Another example of innovation in water processing is the Australian company Biogill, which has developed what the company calls a "nanoceramic membrane" that is conducive to cultivating beneficial bacteria. The bacterially-implanted membrane is effective in cleaning water that cannot be purified using standard treatment methods.[5]

One of the side effects of water pollution is a shortage of drinkable water impacting many communities, especially in developing countries, around the world. A variety of unusual solutions have emerged to address the need for fresh water. The WaterSeer is an unusual device developed by US-based VICI Labs and currently in testing by the National Peace Corps. The device functions much like a well, but instead of drawing water from underground sources it removes water from the atmosphere and collects it in a subterranean chamber so that it can be extracted with a hose. Another American company, Lockheed Martin, has developed a new kind of water filter, the Perforene graphene filter, that could reduce the energy cost of water distillation by as much as 20 percent. This could not only be useful in efforts to purify wastewater but would also reduce the petroleum and other energy used to power traditional wastewater treatment solutions.[6]

Changing Behaviors

The breakdown of the Ocean Cleanup system points to one of the most pressing problems with addressing pollution; changing human behavior. While technology and innovation may be able to address pollution in numerous ways, it is the behavioral patterns of consumers and of corporations that has created the problem, and without addressing these underlying causes, it is impossible to solve the pollution problem. On the most basic level, human culture has become consumer-driven to a large degree and this is especially true in economically powerful nations like the United States. The American people now lead the world in creating solid waste and have fallen well behind many of the world's other developed nations in successful recycling and waste-reduction efforts.

In the 1960s and 1970s, during a surge of environmental consciousness in American popular culture, state governments and the federal bureaucracy adopted some of the first serious environmental laws. This momentum did not last, however, as consumer culture made a massive resurgence in the 1980s. When President Jimmy Carter occupied the White House, he initiated a program to switch the White House and other federal buildings over to solar energy and was also instrumental in efforts to promote recycling and force corporations to use reusable containers and sustainable products. All of these efforts were derailed because of corporate influence. Beverage-making companies donated millions to Republican politicians and defeated a Carter-era law that would have eliminated single-use plastic beverage containers, and the Reagan administration, which had deep financial ties to the oil industry, gutted and dismantled the federal solar energy program. Corporations object to environment-sustainable management because of increased costs, preventing America from making major advancements toward sustainability and reducing pollution.[7]

Ultimately, innovations are only valuable if humanity also makes sacrifices. If societies can reduce pollution levels within cities and towns, then innovative water-cleaning methods might be sufficient to effectively eliminate impact on surrounding water supplies. Likewise, if cities and towns make the changes needed to reduce the production of trash and plastic waste, then efforts to clean oceans and other areas might be productive. As it is, the amount of waste far outpaces the ability to combat the buildup, and the population continues to grow. To effectively eliminate pollution problems, humanity must adopt a suite of solutions that draw upon the very best technological innovations but must also work toward changing consumer and corporate behavior.

Works Used

Becker, Rachel. "Why So Many of Us Wanted to Believe in an Ocean Cleanup System That Just Broke." *The Verge*. Jan. 9, 2019. https://www.theverge.com/2019/1/9/18175940/ocean-cleanup-breaks-plastic-pollution-silicon-valley-boyan-slat-wilson.

Biello, David. "Where Did the Carter White House Solar Panels Go?" *Scientific American*. Aug. 6, 2010. https://www.scientificamerican.com/article/carter-white-house-solar-panel-array/.

Borgobello, Bridget. "Palazzo Italia to Get Air-Purifying Façade for Milan Expo 2015." *New Atlas*. May 23, 2014. https://newatlas.com/palazzo-italia-milan-expo-smog-purifying-facade/32204/.

Brown, Paige. "Catalytic Clothing-Purifying Air Goes Trendy." *Scientific American*. Mar. 21, 2012. https://blogs.scientificamerican.com/guest-blog/catalytic-clothing-purifying-air-goes-trendy/.

Nace, Trevor. "This City Bench Absorbs More Air Pollution Than a Grove of Trees." *Forbes*. Mar. 20, 2018. https://www.forbes.com/sites/trevornace/2018/03/20/this-city-bench-absorbs-more-air-pollution-than-a-grove-of-trees/#c63b776b8d8f.

Shah, Vaidehi. "6 Water-Saving Innovations to Celebrate This World Water Day." *Eco-Business*. Mar. 22, 2017. https://www.eco-business.com/news/6-water-saving-innovations-to-celebrate-this-world-water-day/.

Spinks, Rosie. "Could These Five Innovations Help Solve the Global Water Crisis?" *The Guardian*. Feb. 13, 2017. https://www.theguardian.com/global-development-professionals-network/2017/feb/13/global-water-crisis-innovation-solution.

Notes

1. Nace, "This City Bench Absorbs More Air Pollution Than a Grove of Trees."
2. Borgobello, "Palazzo Italia to Get Air-Purifying Façade for Milan Expo 2015."
3. Brown, "Catalytic Clothing-Purifying Air Goes Trendy."
4. Becker, "Why So Many of Us Wanted to Believe in an Ocean Cleanup System That Just Broke."
5. Shah, "6 Water-Saving Innovations to Celebrate This World Water Day."
6. Spinks, "Could These Five Innovations Help Solve the Global Water Crisis?"
7. Biello, "Where Did the Carter White House Solar Panels Go?"

Helping the Environment, One Small Sensor at a Time

By Ellen Rosen

The New York Times, May 14, 2020

For those working to mitigate climate change—whether globally or hyper-locally—the coronavirus pandemic has raised existential questions. Will the environment still be considered critically important so that philanthropic and venture funding continue to be plentiful?

Several New York City nonprofit organizations, relying on cloud-based technology, are hoping to show that their efforts can, at a relatively modest cost, improve local water and air quality. The Gowanus Canal Conservancy in Brooklyn, the Van Cortlandt Park Alliance in the Bronx and the Hudson Square Business Improvement District in Lower Manhattan are in different stages of piloting a cloud-based service offered by Temboo, itself a TriBeCa-based technology start-up that captures data from sensors to help monitor a range of metrics in environmental and manufacturing sectors.

Temboo does not manufacture the sensors; those come from National Control Devices, an electronics manufacturer based in Osceola, Mo. Instead, it provides a cloud-based platform, known as Kosmos, to capture data they generate. It is what is known as a no-code approach that allows clients to use questions and answers—not unlike TurboTax—to create a system to collect data from sensors.

While Temboo's corporate clients have subscribed to the platform for uses like monitoring manufacturing temperatures, its employees and the chief executive, Trisala Chandaria, have become increasingly interested in how their company could have an environmental impact.

Some of its earliest customers were already doing environmental monitoring with the Kosmos platform for uses such as tracking "soil moisture levels to control irrigation systems more efficiently or setting up temperature and humidity loggers at outdoor sites," said Ms. Chandaria, who is also a co-founder of the company. More environmental sensors appeared on the market, signaling a growing demand. "As a team," she said, "we decided to make a focused push into what we're calling the 'environmental engagement' space," to measure air, water and soil quality.

The goal is to incorporate the sensors as part of a green infrastructure, the use of plants and soil for pollution control in urban centers. It is not a new concept; the Clean Water Act recognized the practice almost 50 years ago. But even as pollution mitigation techniques have become more sophisticated in the intervening years, organic solutions, like plantings, still matter. Tree beds, for example, can still effectively "soak up storm water that flows off the streets or the sidewalk, which is often contaminated from cars and buses," said Andrea Parker, the executive director of the Gowanus Canal Conservancy. "The soil acts like a filter. It's a very effective way of treating that contamination."

Temboo made its first venture into working with nonprofits by attending conferences and cold-calling.

At one gathering, the staff met with representatives of the Gowanus conservancy. The group then purchased sensors to monitor six trees' absorption of polluted rainwater before it could seep into the canal, which has been polluted since the 1800s and is a Superfund site. The small trial, covering the trees on a single block abutting the canal, began last fall. A handful of volunteers oversee moisture levels at individual trees, while one volunteer

The goal is to incorporate sensors as part of a green infrastructure, the use of plants and soil for pollution control in urban centers.

in the neighborhood hosts the so-called gateway device, which receives the sensors' readings and then transmits them to Temboo's platform using Wi-Fi. The trial confirmed that "stewardship of the trees appears to improve storm-water retention," said Amy Motzny, the conservancy's watershed manager.

Even before the preliminary results were in, staff of the Hudson Square district learned of the technology from the Brooklyn organization at the New York City Urban Forest Task Force organized by the Nature Conservancy. The Hudson Square group, devoted to an area west of SoHo, plans to use the sensors with trees to monitor storm water and other concerns like ambient temperature.

"We had landscape architects who hypothesized that the 250 existing trees capture 12 Olympic-sized pools of storm water annually, could lower temperatures on the blocks where the trees are planted by up to 5 degrees and capture the carbon-dioxide emissions generated by 35 round trips by plane to Los Angeles," said Ellen Baer, president and chief executive of the Hudson Square Business Improvement District. Those estimates are just that, and Ms. Baer said installing sensors in new trees set to be planted this year would help quantify these figures.

Temboo sought out the Van Cortlandt alliance, an organization focusing on the park of the same name in the Bronx. John Butler, an ecological project manager, was intrigued; he thought that the sensors could help measure debris and emissions flowing from nearby roads into the park. The alliance was already monitoring water quality in the park's namesake lake as well as Tibbetts Brook, which runs through the park, the city's third largest, but he now plans to install sensors in the underground pipes that carry the tainted water as well.

"With only a small staff, we can't collect the data during a storm, but with sensors it could be amazing," Mr. Butler said. "We would use this data to show that we need to make changes to these pipes and why we need to install green infrastructure so the polluted water can be captured before it flows into the lake." While the organization has not determined a solution, one possibility, he said, was to "daylight" the brook to bring it to the surface, rather than divert it through the old pipes, and create a new wetland to absorb the water before it can pollute.

The coronavirus outbreak may delay the planting of new trees in Hudson Square as well as installing the sensors there and in Van Cortlandt Park. But the pandemic has also caused Temboo to "have the conversation about what can we learn," Ms. Chandaria said.

"We've designed our systems for efficiency rather than resiliency," she continued. "We've had to decide if we should reprioritize the features we will roll out. We realize it will be hard to deploy sensors during this time of social distancing, so we have to adapt to prioritize features that are less dependent on the sensors. Some features have come from volunteers—like photos and notes—but on our own road map, how do we include public data so it supplements what's being measured?"

She added, as an example, that the Environmental Protection Agency measured a range of indicators and that "we've started looking at their health data to see if we can relate it to our data." New data can enter their Kosmos platform, she said, so that "people can mix and match data with public data streams."

"We had planned on introducing this ability later on in the year, but because of the crisis we are front-loading it."

Ms. Chandaria is also mulling over how sensors could become a revenue source for the nonprofits—in essence making them more sustainable. If, for example, local volunteers monitor the data and take responsibility for inspecting and watering trees as necessary, as is done in Gowanus, could the nonprofit get grants or even municipal funding to provide services that city governments cannot?

If the Gowanus pilot is any indication, it should not be difficult to enlist more local residents. According to Ms. Parker, "two volunteers are in the tech industry, and they're excited about the interface with technology and are enjoying the livestream of data." And, she added, "they also make decisions of their own stewardship such as whether they need to water the trees to help the infiltration rate."

Print Citations

CMS: Rosen, Ellen. "Helping the Environment, One Small Sensor at a Time." In *The Reference Shelf: Pollution,* edited by Micah L. Issitt, 133-135. Amenia, NY: Grey House Publishing, 2020.

MLA: Rosen, Ellen. "Helping the Environment, One Small Sensor at a Time." *The Reference Shelf: Pollution,* edited by Micah L. Issitt, Grey Housing Publishing, 2020, pp. 133-135.

APA: Rosen, E. (2020). Helping the environment, one small sensor at a time. In Micah L. Issitt (Ed.), *The reference shelf: Pollution* (pp. 133-135). Amenia, NY: Grey Housing Publishing.

Ocean Cleanup Won't Turn a Profit, But We Should Still Do It

By Peter King

The Conversation, October 21, 2018

A novel "floating pipe" to recover plastic from the ocean has just arrived on its maiden voyage to the Great Pacific Garbage Patch. Run by Dutch start-up Ocean Cleanup, the scheme involves a 600m-long floating pipe connected to a net, which herds plastic into place before it is gathered and taken to shore by specialist boats.

The question of why we should bother to clean up the oceans may seem obvious to you but, as an economist who studies these things, I like to put a number on it. We can therefore say that plastic in the ocean has a direct financial impact through things such as lost tourism, damaged ships or fewer fish to catch. But it also has a wider and harder to quantify economic impact on lost marine life or reduced beach and water quality.

These damages, estimated at US$1.25 billion annually, imply that recovering marine plastics is worthwhile. But my research suggests that it might not be financially viable to do so.

This is partly because the clean-up is so expensive. Unsurprisingly, towing a massive boom out to the middle of the ocean and then periodically transporting plastics to and from it is not cheap.

The Ocean Cleanup's own 2014 feasibility study suggested that, once a full fleet of 100km of these floating barriers was deployed at a cost of US$372.73m (currency converted by myself in August 2018), it would collect plastic at around US$5.32 per kilogram.

This wouldn't be a problem if discarded plastic was more valuable. The scheme could even pay for itself. But the clean-up will remain unprofitable for the time being because the market price for discarded plastic remains incredibly low. I looked at four possible options for recovered plastic:

1. Landfill: This is the easiest option although it leads to actual net losses rather than any benefit.

Revenue per kg: -$0.12

---

2. Incineration: Burning all waste generates electricity which is reportedly as much as 60% cleaner than a fossil fuel equivalent. However, this negates the possibility of recycling or reusing the plastics.

Revenue per kg: $0.10

3. Pyrolysis: Similar to incineration, except the plastic is heated in the absence of oxygen, so it doesn't burn. Instead, the process generates oils which can be refined and sold. However, the viability of pyrolysis is dependent on economies of scale which may not suit it to the infrequent collection of marine plastics. Furthermore, at a low level, it is unlikely that the generated oil from plastics can be price competitive with conventional oil sources.

Revenue per kg: $0.27

4. Recycling: This is the preferred option, as it is a more efficient use of existing resources. But volatile recycled plastic prices and low virgin plastic prices suggest that this, too, is unlikely to be a profitable option.

Revenue per kg: variable, but a weighted average of $0.15 is a reasonable assumption

All this means it costs more than $5 to gather a kilo of plastic from the ocean, while that same plastic will only be valued at—at best—30 cents. With about 8 billion kilos (8,000 tonnes) of plastic added to the ocean each year, the costs—and losses—involved are huge.

Costs Will Decline in the Long Term

Of course, such a massive loss is not likely to persist in the long term. For instance, increasing oil prices will push up the price of virgin plastics hence making recycling a more valuable option. Furthermore, the high cost expectations are primarily due to this being the first system of its type. With further experience, research and development in recovering debris at sea, it is likely that a lower-cost method will arise. However, there is no immediate indication of such improvements, and so big losses are expected to persist in the short to medium term.

> **The international nature of plastic pollution suggests no single government is going to foot the bill.**

The financial loss contrasts with the economic benefits of recovering marine plastics. Even conservative underestimates of the costs of marine plastics suggest annual damages to be in the billions.

Using estimates of how much plastic is in the ocean, I was able to estimate that removing each kilogram would lead to a net benefit of at least US$7 and as much as US$38. But that still leaves us with a direct financial loss of nearly US$5 per kilogram recovered, versus a more than US$7 net benefit to society for every kilogram recovered.

Unprofitable... but Imperative

So we are at an impasse. It is nowhere near profitable to recover marine plastics, yet it is imperative to do so. Thankfully, a few solutions are at hand.

The first is crowdfunding. This avenue worked before for the scheme in question which managed to raise more than $2m in just 100 days. But there are doubts about how viable such a fickle and inconsistent funding source is for a longer-running scheme that would operate at a global scale.

Philanthropy is another option. Conceivably, with the support of just a few wealthy benefactors, viable ocean clean-up could be a reality. However, it is unclear whether leaving ocean clean-up to the whim of a few individuals is a sustainable model in the longer term.

Finally, the international nature of plastic pollution suggests no single government is going to foot the bill—especially if all the financial benefits are privately appropriated. However, one suggestion is that if taxpayers are already paying environmental charges aimed at reducing plastic pollution, such as the plastic bag tax or proposed latte levy, then perhaps these revenues could be earmarked to fund the scheme.

So future policymakers must pay particular attention to the various mechanisms and agreements that may bridge the gap between financial losses and economic benefits. Indeed, evidence suggests a healthy degree of public support for cleaning up the environment, but whether the public feels strongly enough to support efforts via crowdfunding or earmarked taxes remains to be seen.

Plastic causes $13 in damages per kilogram per year. The race is on to determine how we can clean up the world's oceans without bankrupting ourselves.

Print Citations

CMS: King, Peter. "Ocean Cleanup Won't Turn a Profit, But We Should Still Do It." In *The Reference Shelf: Pollution,* edited by Micah L. Issitt, 136-138. Amenia, NY: Grey House Publishing, 2020.

MLA: King, Peter. "Ocean Cleanup Won't Turn a Profit, But We Should Still Do It." *The Reference Shelf: Pollution,* edited by Micah L. Issitt, Grey Housing Publishing, 2020, pp. 136-138.

APA: King, P. (2020). Ocean Cleanup Won't Turn a Profit, But We Should Still Do It. In Micah L. Issitt (Ed.), *The reference shelf: Pollution* (pp. 136-138). Amenia, NY: Grey Housing Publishing.

China Could Wash Away Smog with Artificial Rain Storms from Skyscrapers

By Kelsey Campbell-Dollaghan
Gizmodo, January 20, 2014

Airborne pollution is a major issue in China, with local hospitals opening up "smog clinics" and waves of city-dwellers migrating to more rural areas to escape. While Chinese officials are pursuing "cloud seeding" as a way to control pollution, a Zhejiang University professor thinks he has a better idea: Sprinklers. Big ones.

Yu Shaocai is a former U.S. Environmental Protection Agency employee and an expert on "wet deposition," a process by which falling raindrops or snowflakes "scavenge" aerosol particles from the air. In other words, they collect and deposit the polluted particles on the ground. This why the air is usually clearer after a rainy day.

In an article published in the January issue of *Environmental Chemistry Letters,* Shaocai proposes a novel way to kickstart wet deposition in polluted cities:

> **Most urban pollution drifts below 300 feet, which means existing towers offer the perfect platform for wet deposition.**

By faking it with geoengineered urban infrastructure. In simpler terms, Shaocai's plan involves attaching giant sprinklers, like showerheads, to the exterior of skyscrapers, and spraying water into the atmosphere above heavily-polluted cities to clear out toxins and gases.

As you might expect, Shaocai has his detractors. Speaking to the *South China Morning Post,* one scientist questions where the water would come from and how it would be recycled, but then grudgingly admits that "assuming his team can find a system that works, and they've done enough economic analysis and considered the handling of water resources, this could be a viable option."

Then, of course, there's the cost of retrofitting skyscrapers with watering devices, not to mention designing a system that's safe during storms and high winds. Or engineering a system smart enough to not overwater, or freeze up on cold days.

In short, this a theoretical paper in a chemistry journal—not a workable plan. Yet.

Shaocai told the SCMP that he and his students plan to carry out tests at Zhejiang University, first, and then in Hangzhou. In his paper, he imagines the architectural implications of attaching sprinkler systems to Beijing's CCTV building or Shanghai Dongfang Tower. . . .

Shaocai's plan sounds (and looks) like the stuff of turn-of-the-century science fiction. But it's actually fairly logical. Most urban pollution drifts below 300 feet, which means existing towers offer the perfect platform for wet deposition. And, of course, skyscrapers are usually located in parts of cities where humans spend the most time commuting—so it makes sense that man-made "rainouts" would need to mirror them on the map.

In December, the China Meteorological Administration announced a $277 billion plan to begin large-scale cloud seeding around Chinese cities, clearing pollution by "firing rockets carrying a payload of silver iodide particles into the clouds." But there are questions about whether cloud-seeding will actually work to spur wet deposition, since existing snow and rainfall should already be doing that job.

Whether or not Shaocai ever makes it off the drawing board, it's really cool to see how architecture—even the sort most associated with vanity and excess, the skyscraper—could serve secondary and tertiary urban functions in the near future. When humans first began building tall buildings, we imagined all kinds of future purposed for them: The Empire State Building was supposed to have its own Zeppelin tethering dock; other skyscrapers were supposed to support whole airplane runways.

None of those futures ever came to pass—but it's amazing to see other, totally unexpected ones emerge.

Print Citations

CMS: Campbell-Dollaghan, Kelsey. "China Could Wash Away Smog with Artificial Rain Storms from Skyscrapers." In *The Reference Shelf: Pollution,* edited by Micah L. Issitt, 139-140. Amenia, NY: Grey House Publishing, 2020.

MLA: Campbell-Dollaghan, Kelsey. "China Could Wash Away Smog with Artificial Rain Storms from Skyscrapers." *The Reference Shelf: Pollution,* edited by Micah L. Issitt, Grey Housing Publishing, 2020, pp. 139-140.

APA: Campbell-Dollaghan, K. (2020). China could wash away smog with artificial rain storms from skyscrapers. In Micah L. Issitt (Ed.), *The reference shelf: Pollution* (pp. 139-140). Amenia, NY: Grey Housing Publishing.

Pulling CO2 Out of the Air and Using It Could Be a Trillion-Dollar Business

By David Roberts
Vox, November 22, 2019

Scientists generally estimate that to hold the rise in global average temperature to 1.5 degrees Celsius over the preindustrial baseline—a "safe" level of warming—humanity must stabilize the atmospheric concentration of carbon dioxide at around 350 parts per million.

This year, we reached about 410 ppm. There is already too much CO2 in the atmosphere. At this point, to truly vouchsafe a secure climate for future generations, we don't just have to reduce emissions; we have to pull some CO2 out of the atmosphere.

Given that global carbon emissions are still rising and there are hundreds of gigatons on the way from existing fossil fuel infrastructure, almost every model used by the Intergovernmental Panel on Climate Change (IPCC) that shows us reaching a safe climate involves burying gigatons of CO2, so-called "negative emissions."

There are many forms of negative emissions, but most likely the only way to remove *enough* CO2 will be to pull it directly out of the air and bury it underground in saline aquifers, a process known as carbon capture and sequestration (CCS). With CCS, CO2 is treated as a waste product that has to be disposed of properly, just as we treat sewage and so many other pollution hazards.

How much CO2 will need to be buried? Obviously, it's impossible to know in advance; IPCC models vary in how fast they show emissions falling. The faster and sooner emissions fall, the less CCS will be necessary. The slower and later they fall, the more that will be needed.

A 2017 paper in *Nature Climate Change* estimates the total "mitigation burden"—that is the total amount of emissions that need to be avoided between now and 2050 to stay under 2 degree—at 800 gigatons. (Though the IPCC says 1.5 degrees is the truly safe target, many scientists believe it's unachievable; 2 degrees remains an extremely ambitious target.) The paper estimates that even if emission reductions are successful, between 120–160 gigatons will need to be sequestered during that period.

Another way of saying that is, even given optimistic assumptions about decarbonization, we'll probably end up emitting a lot more than our carbon budget, so we'll need to bury between 100 and 200 gigatons of CO_2 to get back within it. And, of course, we'll have to bury hundreds of gigatons more in the years after 2050.

To give a sense of scale, that means by 2030 humanity needs to be compressing, transporting, and burying an amount of CO_2, by volume, that is two to four times the amount of fluids that the global oil and gas industry deals with today. To build an industry of that scale, by that date, we need to begin today, with large-scale research and deployment. The price of capturing CO_2 from the air needs to be driven down quickly.

But there's a problem: Burying CO_2 has no short-term economic benefits. In the absence of a fairly stiff price on carbon, meant to put a value on its long-term benefits, CCS doesn't pencil out. There's no incentive for companies to do it and thus no incentive to get better at carbon capture.

The easy solution to this dilemma would be a global price on carbon, but that doesn't appear to be happening. So how, in the absence of a carbon price, can the carbon capture industry get going?

Here's one idea: For a while at least, rather than burying the carbon, the companies capturing it could sell it.

Utilizing CO2 Could Provide a Push for Carbon Capture

Carbon dioxide is a commodity with some value. It is used, both directly and as a feedstock, by a range of industries and has been for over a century.

Most CO_2 used by industries today is a byproduct of fossil fuel processes, often from natural gas or coal-fueled plants making ammonia; that is it comes from below the Earth's surface. Just like burning fossil fuels, it transfers CO_2 from the geosphere to the atmosphere.

But if CO_2 pulled out of the air became more plentiful and cheaper, it could begin competing with terrestrial CO_2. In theory, any industry that uses carbon from under the ground—for fuel, beverages, directly in industrial processes, as a feedstock to create other products, or whatever—could switch to air-captured CO_2.

> **Rather than burying the carbon, the companies capturing it could sell it.**

Using CO_2 from the air for products and services is known as carbon capture and utilization (CCU). By some estimates, it's a potentially $1 trillion market by 2030. And it could have two broad benefits.

First, it could reduce CO_2 emissions, in part by sequestering some carbon permanently in durable products and in part by substituting for carbon-intensive processes, thus avoiding emissions that would have otherwise occurred.

To be clear, CCU will never reduce enough CO_2 to avoid the need for CCS (i.e., burying carbon). Not even close. The tonnage of CO_2 humanity emits simply dwarfs the tonnage of carbon-based products it consumes.

But CCU could be a helpful tool in the decarbonization tool belt. As one recent paper put it, "Each atom of C we can recycle is an atom of fossil carbon left in the underground for next generations that will not reach the atmosphere today." By one optimistic estimate, CCU could reduce up to 10 percent of total global emissions by 2030.

Second, demand for CO2 driven by CCU could provide early market pull, helping to get carbon capture technology scaled up and its costs pushed down, so that it is ready when policymakers finally get around to supporting CCS in earnest. It could serve as an "on ramp" to CCS.

A Guide to the Complex and Confusing World of Carbon Utilization

This is a hot and rapidly developing area in the climate and energy world. There are all sorts of research going on into novel uses of CO2, all sorts of pilot projects underway, all sorts of startups popping up, and all sorts of confusing information and hype floating around. So let's see if we can sort it out.

Here's how this series of posts will go. In this post, we'll take a brief look at the two major sources of industrial carbon capture and the basic ways CO2 is currently used by industry, just to get oriented.

In the second post, we will discuss the vexed subject of enhanced oil recovery (EOR), which is by far the largest current industrial use of CO2.

In the third post, we will take a closer look at the top non-EOR markets for CO2, like building materials and fuels, and their total potential, in both economic and carbon terms.

And in the final post, we'll contemplate the road forward for CCU, what kinds of supportive policies it requires, and, taking a step back, the right way to see it in the overall context of the climate fight.

It's going to be fun! You'll never see CO2 quite the same way again.

Varieties of Carbon Capture

First, let's get clear on what I mean when I talk about standing up an industrial carbon capture industry.

A wide variety of "natural" processes absorb and sequester carbon, on land (forests and soil), on the coasts (wetlands and mangroves), and in the ocean. The carbon-absorbing capacity of those processes can be enhanced with clever human management—e.g., the US Geological Service's LandCarbon program—and they can play a large role in the climate fight.

But in these posts, we will instead be discussing industrial carbon capture, machines built to absorb CO2 from the air via chemical reactions. We won't get into the various chemistries and technologies involved (there are many, and they are complicated), but it is worth keeping in mind one distinction.

CO2 can either be pulled out of flue gases—waste streams produced by power generation or other industrial processes—or it can be pulled out of the ambient air through a process known as direct air capture (DAC). Each has its advantages and disadvantages.

The great advantage of drawing from flue gases is that the CO2 is concentrated, roughly one molecule out of every 10, whereas in the ambient air, it is one molecule out of every 2,500. With the laws of chemistry being what they are, it's always going to require less energy to draw a material from an already-concentrated source. On a raw commodity price basis, CO_2 from flue gases will likely always be cheaper than CO_2 produced by DAC.

But DAC has advantages of its own. First, it is geographically agnostic. It does not need to be attached to anything or built in any particular place. CO_2 is equally concentrated in the air everywhere in the world, so DAC can be built anywhere in the world, wherever the CO_2 is needed, eliminating transportation costs. It is smaller, more modular, and more adaptable.

Second, unlike every other form of carbon capture, terrestrial or industrial, DAC is limited only by costs. It can scale up to any size, depending only on our willingness to spend money on it. That's why many in the field believe DAC to be the most promising negative-emissions technology in the long term.

(NB: there are companies like Global Thermostat with technologies they claim can capture carbon from either source.)

As we will see, various options for CCU may be better suited to one form of capture or the other.

The Use of CO2 and Its Potential

With all that background, let's have a look at the ways CO_2 is currently used.

Starting at the bottom: CO_2 can be used directly, in greenhouses, to carbonate beverages, or for enhanced oil recovery (the largest current use), or it can be transformed, via a wide variety of chemical processes, into materials or feedstocks. One of the chemical conversions with the biggest potential, up at the top, is combining CO_2 with hydrogen to make synthetic hydrocarbon fuels. . . .

Some of these processes and products are further along in market development than others; some have larger carbon mitigation potential than others; some have larger total market potential than others. (We'll look at all of that more closely in the third post.)

One distinction to keep in mind for now has to do with how long each of these options sequesters CO_2.

For most of them, it's a relatively short time. For instance, if captured CO_2 is used to make synthetic fuels, the fuels are then burned, at which point the CO_2 is released back into the atmosphere. It's carbon recycling (or upcycling), not carbon sequestration.

Enhanced oil recovery can be done in concert with permanent geological carbon sequestration, but it rarely is today. (We'll look at that more closely in the second post.)

Of the various other categories of CCU, only construction materials (and possibly new materials like carbon fiber) can claim to sequester CO_2 semi-permanently. When you inject CO_2 into concrete, the concrete is then used in a building which could last up to a century; then, if the building comes down, the concrete can be broken up and re-used. The CO_2 stays put, chemically bonded.

This distinction matters in contemplating the total mitigation potential of CCU. Only a small slice of it can ever claim to be carbon-negative; its sequestration potential is limited. For the most part, its benefit will come from replacing carbon-intensive processes with carbon-neutral ones, avoiding carbon emissions. (And even that potential may be limited; more on that in the fourth post.)

All this means, again, that CCU will never substitute for CCS. At best it will help lay the foundation for CCS. . . .

It is worth noting that these optimistic projections are not universally shared; the roadmap's estimate of mitigation potential is at the high end of recent studies. A 2005 IPCC assessment concluded gloomily that "the scale of the use of captured CO2 in industrial processes is too small, the storage times too short, and the energy balance too unfavourable for industrial uses of CO2 to become significant as a means of mitigating climate change."

Still, a lot has changed since 2005. Renewable energy has gotten cheaper and CO2 conversion has improved. At the very least, CCU is one of many potentially carbon abating technologies that deserves much more attention and support than it is currently getting from policymakers.

Politics do not exactly encourage long-term thinking, but 2050 isn't that far away, and 2030 is closer still. Holding temperature "well below" 2 degrees, the UN goal, does not just mean reaching net-zero emissions by 2050, as most of the Democratic candidates for president now support. It also means building the capacity to bury hundreds of gigatons of carbon. Insofar as CCU can help get that going—an open question, for now—it is worth pursuing.

Print Citations

CMS: Roberts, David. "Pulling CO2 Out of the Air and Using It Could Be a Trillion-Dollar Business." In *The Reference Shelf: Pollution,* edited by Micah L. Issitt, 141-145. Amenia, NY: Grey House Publishing, 2020.

MLA: Roberts, David. "Pulling CO2 Out of the Air and Using It Could Be a Trillion-Dollar Business." *The Reference Shelf: Pollution,* edited by Micah L. Issitt, Grey Housing Publishing, 2020, pp. 141-145.

APA: Roberts, D. (2020). Pulling CO2 out of the air and using it could be a trillion-dollar business. In Micah L. Issitt (Ed.), *The reference shelf: Pollution* (pp. 141-145). Amenia, NY: Grey Housing Publishing.

This Bicycle Will Clean Polluted Air While You Pedal

By Nick Mafi
Architectural Digest, May 17, 2017

As urban environments grow, particularly in emerging markets such as China, Brazil, and India, city smog is increasingly becoming a public health concern. Indeed, according to the World Health Organization, around 3 million deaths a year worldwide are attributable to air pollution. That's one of many reasons why the Dutch artist and innovator Dan Roosegaarde has taken it upon himself to design a series of products to help curb the growing problems stemming from pollution. Last fall, Roosegaarde unveiled a series of 23-foot-high towers that, in essence, operate as a massive air purifier. But Roosegaarde wasn't content only designing pollution-curbing buildings. He felt there was more he could do. And he was right.

> **The implications could be enormous, particularly in urban environments where bike lanes are interwoven within the grid.**

The Dutch innovator recently unveiled a concept bicycle that, true to form, cleans polluted air while the rider pedals. Dubbed the Smog Free bicycle, the invention works by sucking the polluted air into a contraption located on the front of the bike, cleaning it through a filtration system, then releasing the fresh air—all while the rider is pedaling through the streets. The idea has been supported by various factions of the Chinese government, providing Roosegaarde the push needed to get the concept bicycle through its first stages of development. The implications could be enormous, particularly in urban environments where bike lanes are interwoven within the grid (including major cities such as New York, Berlin, Buenos Aires, and Beijing), and where bike-sharing programs are on the rise. But for now, with the backing of its government, it's in China where the innovative design is being most heralded. "Beijing used to be an iconic bicycle city," said Roosegaarde in a statement. "We want to bring back the bicycle—not only as a cultural icon of China, but also as the next step towards smog-free cities."

Print Citations

CMS: Mafi, Nick. "This Bicycle Will Clean Polluted Air While You Pedal." In *The Reference Shelf: Pollution,* edited by Micah L. Issitt, 146-147. Amenia, NY: Grey House Publishing, 2020.

MLA: Mafi, Nick. "This Bicycle Will Clean Polluted Air While You Pedal." *The Reference Shelf: Pollution,* edited by Micah L. Issitt, Grey Housing Publishing, 2020, pp. 146-147.

APA: Mafi, N. (2020). This bicycle will clean polluted air while you pedal. In Micah L. Issitt (Ed.), *The reference shelf: Pollution* (pp. 146-147). Amenia, NY: Grey Housing Publishing.

What If Air Conditioners Could Help Save the Planet Instead of Destroying It?

By Matt Simon
Wired, April 30, 2019

Earth's climate is full of terrifying feedback loops: Decreased rainfall raises the risk of wildfires, which release yet more carbon dioxide. A warming Arctic could trigger the release of long-frozen methane, which would heat the planet even faster than carbon. A lesser-known climate feedback loop, though, is likely mere feet from where you're sitting: the air conditioner. Use of the energy-intensive appliance causes emissions that contribute to higher global temperatures, which means we're all using AC more, producing more emissions and more warming.

But what if we could weaponize air conditioning units to help pull carbon dioxide out of the atmosphere instead? According to a new paper in *Nature Communications*, it's feasible. Using technology currently in development, AC units in skyscrapers and even your home could get turned into machines that not only capture CO_2, but transform the stuff into a fuel for powering vehicles that are difficult to electrify, like cargo ships. The concept, called crowd oil, is still theoretical and faces many challenges. But in these desperate times, crowd oil might have a place in the fight to curb climate change.

The problem with air conditioners isn't just that they suck up lots of energy but that they also emit heat. "When you run an air conditioning system, you don't get anything for nothing," says materials chemist Geoffrey Ozin of the University of Toronto, coauthor on the new paper. "If you cool something, you heat something, and that heat goes into the cities." Their use exacerbates the heat island effect of cities—lots of concrete soaks up lots of heat, which a city releases well after the sun sets.

To retrofit an air conditioner to capture CO_2 and turn it into fuel, you'd need a rather extensive overhaul of the components. Meaning, you wouldn't just be able to ship a universal device for folks to bolt onto their units. First of all, you'd need to incorporate a filter that would absorb CO_2 and water from the air. You'd also need to include an electrolyzer to strip the oxygen molecule from H_2O to get H_2, which you'd then combine with CO_2 to get hydrocarbon fuels. "Everyone can have their own oil well, basically," Ozin says.

The researchers' analysis found that the Frankfurt Fair Tower in Germany (chosen by lead author Roland Dittmeyer of the Karlsruhe Institute of Technology, by the way, because of its land-mark status in the city's sky-line), with a total volume of about 200,000 cubic meters, could capture 1.5 metric tons of CO_2 per hour and produce

> **The problem with air conditioners isn't just that they suck up lots of energy but that they also emit heat.**

up to 4,000 metric tons of fuel a year. By comparison, the first commercial "direct air capture" plant, built by Climeworks in Switzerland, captures 900 metric tons of CO_2 per year, about 10 times less, Dittmeyer says. An apartment building with five or six units could capture 0.5 kg of CO_2 an hour with this proposed system.

Theoretically, anywhere you have an air conditioner, you have a way to make synthetic fuel. "The important point is that you can convert the CO_2 into a liquid product onsite, and there are pilot-scale plants that can do that," says Dittmeyer, who is working on one with colleagues that is able to produce 10 liters a day. They hope to multiply that output by a factor of 20 in the next two years.

For this process to be carbon neutral, though, all those souped-up air condi-tioners would need to be powered with renewables, because burning the synthetic fuel would also produce emissions. To address that problem, Dittmeyer proposes turning whole buildings into solar panels—placing them not just on rooftops but potentially coating facades and windows with ultrathin, largely transparent panels. "It's like a tree—the skyscraper or house you live in produces a chemical reaction," Dittmeyer says. "It's like the glucose that a tree is producing." That kind of building transformation won't happen overnight, of course, a reminder that installing carbon scrubbers is only ever one piece of the solution.

Scaling up the technology to many buildings and cities poses yet more chal-lenges. Among them, how to store and then collect all that accumulated fuel. The idea is for trucks to gather and transport the stuff to a facility, or in some cases when the output is greater, pipelines would be built. That means both retrofitting a whole lot of AC units (the cost of which isn't yet clear, since the technology isn't finalized yet), and building out an infrastructure to ferry that fuel around for use in industry.

"Carbon-neutral hydrocarbon fuels from electricity can help solve two of our biggest energy challenges: managing intermittent renewables and decarbonizing the hard-to-electrify parts of transportation and industry," says David Keith, acting chief scientist of Carbon Engineering, which is developing much larger stand-alone devices for sucking CO_2 out of the air and storing it, known as carbon capture and storage, or CCS. "While I may be biased by my work with Carbon Engineering, I am deeply skeptical about a distributed solution. Economies of scale can't be wished away. There's a reason we have huge wind turbines, a reason we don't feed yard waste into all-in-one nano-scale pulp-and-paper mills."

Any carbon capture technology also faces the sticky problem of the moral hazard. The concern is that negative emissions technologies, like what Carbon Engineering is working on, and neutral emissions approaches, like this new framework, distract from the most critical objective for fighting climate change: Reducing emissions, and fast. Some would argue that all money and time must go toward developing technologies that will allow any industry or vehicle to become carbon neutral or even carbon negative.

This new framework isn't meant to be a cure-all for climate change. After all, for it to be truly carbon neutral it'd need to run entirely on renewable energy. To that end, it would presumably encourage the development of those energy technologies. (The building-swaddling photovoltaics that Dittmeyer envisions are just becoming commercially available.) "I don't think it would be ethically wrong to pursue this," says environmental social scientist Selma L'Orange Seigo of ETH Zurich, who wasn't involved in this research but has studied public perception of CCS. "It would be ethically wrong to *only* pursue this."

One potential charm of this AC carbon-capture scenario, though, is that it attempts to address a common problem faced by CCS systems, which is that someone has to pay for it. That is, a business that captures and locks away its CO_2 has nothing to sell. AC units that turn CO_2 into fuel, though, would theoretically come with a revenue stream. "There›s definitely a market," Seigo says. "That›s one of the big issues with CCS."

Meanwhile, people will continue running their energy-hungry air conditioners. For sensitive populations like the elderly, access to AC during heat waves is a life or death matter: Consider that the crippling heat wave that struck Europe in August 2003 killed 35,000 people, and these sorts of events are growing more frequent and intense as the planet warms as a whole. A desert nation like Saudi Arabia, by the way, devotes a stunning 70 percent of its energy to powering AC units; in the near future, a whole lot of other places on Earth are going to feel a lot more like Saudi Arabia.

So no, carbon-capturing AC units won't save the world on their own. But they could act as a valuable intermittent renewable as researchers figure out how to get certain industries and vehicles to go green.

Print Citations

CMS: Simon, Matt. "What If Air Conditioners Could Help Save the Planet Instead of Destroying It?" In *The Reference Shelf: Pollution,* edited by Micah L. Issitt, 148-150. Amenia, NY: Grey House Publishing, 2020.

MLA: Simon, Matt. "What If Air Conditioners Could Help Save the Planet Instead of Destroying It?" *The Reference Shelf: Pollution,* edited by Micah L. Issitt, Grey Housing Publishing, 2020, pp. 148-150.

APA: Simon, M. (2020). What if air conditioners could help save the planet instead of destroying it? In Micah L. Issitt (Ed.), *The reference shelf: Pollution* (pp. 148-150). Amenia, NY: Grey Housing Publishing.

Bibliography

"Animals Need the Dark." *NPS*. National Park Service. Apr. 19, 2018. https://www. nps.gov/articles/nocturnal_earthnight.htm.

"Basic Information about Landfills." *EPA*. 2020. https://www.epa.gov/landfills/basic-information-about-landfills.

Becker, Rachel. "Why So Many of Us Wanted to Believe in an Ocean Cleanup System That Just Broke." *The Verge*. Jan. 9, 2019. https://www.theverge. com/2019/1/9/18175940/ocean-cleanup-breaks-plastic-pollution-silicon-valley-boyan-slat-wilson.

Biello, David. "Where Did the Carter White House Solar Panels Go?" *Scientific American*. Aug. 6, 2010. https://www.scientificamerican.com/article/carter-white-house-solar-panel-array/.

Biggers, Alana, and Jamie Eske. "The Effects of Going More Than 24 Hours without Sleep." *Medical News Today*. Mar. 26, 2019. https://www.medicalnewstoday. com/articles/324799.

Boissoneault, Lorraine. "The Cuyahoga River Caught Fire at Least a Dozen Times, but No One Cared Until 1969." *Smithsonian Magazine*. June 19, 2019. https:// www.smithsonianmag.com/history/cuyahoga-river-caught-fire-least-dozen-times-no-one-cared-until-1969-180972444/.

Borgobello, Bridget. "Palazzo Italia to Get Air-Purifying Façade for Milan Expo 2015." *New Atlas*. May 23, 2014. https://newatlas.com/palazzo-italia-milan-expo-smog-purifying-facade/32204/.

Bradford, Alina. "Pollution Facts & Types of Pollution." *Live Science*. Feb. 28, 2018. https://www.livescience.com/22728-pollution-facts.html.

Brevik, Eric C. "A Brief History of Soil Science." *Land Use, Land Cover and Soil Sciences*. https://www.eolss.net/Sample-Chapters/C19/E1-05-07-01.pdf.

Brown, Paige. "Catalytic Clothing-Purifying Air Goes Trendy." *Scientific American*. Mar. 21, 2012. https://blogs.scientificamerican.com/guest-blog/catalytic-clothing-purifying-air-goes-trendy/.

Chatterjee, Rhitu. "Where Did Agriculture Begin? Oh Boy, It's Complicated." *NPR*. July 15, 2016. https://www.npr.org/sections/thesalt/2016/07/15/485722228/ where-did-agriculture-begin-oh-boy-its-complicated.

"Clean Air Act Title IV—Noise Pollution." *EPA*. 2020. https://www.epa.gov/clean-air-act-overview/clean-air-act-title-iv-noise-pollution.

"Covid-19 Lockdowns Significantly Impacting Global Air Quality." *Science Daily*. May 11, 2020. https://www.sciencedaily.com/releases/2020/05/200511124444. htm.

Dunaway, Finis. "The 'Crying Indian' Ad That Fooled the Environmental Movement." *Chicago Tribune*. Nov. 21, 2017. https://www.chicagotribune.com/

opinion/commentary/ct-perspec-indian-crying-environment-ads-pollution-1123-20171113-story.html.

"Environmental Impact of the Petroleum Industry." *EPA*. Environmental Protection Agency. June 2003. https://cfpub.epa.gov/ncer_abstracts/index.cfm/fuseaction/display.files/fileID/14522.

Eschner, Kat. "Is Light Pollution Really Pollution?" *Smithsonian*. June 1, 2017. https://www.smithsonianmag.com/smart-news/light-pollution-really-pollution-180963474/.

Fisher, Len. "How Much Salt Is in a Human Body?" *Science Focus*. https://www.sciencefocus.com/the-human-body/how-much-salt-is-in-a-human-body/.

Freinkel, Susan. "A Brief History of Plastic's Conquest of the World." *Scientific American*. May 29, 2011. https://www.scientificamerican.com/article/a-brief-history-of-plastic-world-conquest/.

Goines, Lisa, and Louis Hagler. "Noise Pollution: A Modern Plague." *Southern Medical Journal*. Vol. 100, Mar. 2007.

Helmenstine, Anne Marie. "The Chemical Composition of Air." July 7, 2019. https://www.thoughtco.com/chemical-composition-of-air-604288.

Helmenstine, Anne Marie. "How Much of Your Body Is Water?" *Thought Co*. Feb. 11, 2020.   https://www.thoughtco.com/how-much-of-your-body-is-water-609406.

Hirst, K. Kris. "The Discovery of Fire." *Thought Co*. May 4, 2019. https://www.thoughtco.com/the-discovery-of-fire-169517.

"Historical Perspective on Air Pollution Control," in *Safe Design and Operation of Process Vents and Emission Control Systems*. Center for Chemical Process Safety. New York: John Wiley & Sons, Inc., 2006.

"History of the Clean Water Act," *EPA*. 2020. https://www.epa.gov/laws-regulations/history-clean-water-act.

"History of Plastic." *Dartmouth University*. http://www.dartmouth.edu/~iispacs/Education/EARS18/Plastic_2013/History%20of%20Plastics/History%20of%20Plastics.html.

Holden, Emily. "US Produces Far More Waste and Recycles Far Less of It Than Other Developed Countries." *The Guardian*. July 3, 2019. https://www.theguardian.com/us-news/2019/jul/02/us-plastic-waste-recycling.

"Hugh Hammond Bennett." *Natural Resources Conservation Service*. USDA.   https://www.nrcs.usda.gov/wps/portal/nrcs/detail/national/about/history/?cid=stelprdb1044395.

Knight, Laurence. "A Brief History of Plastics, Natural and Synthetic." *BBC*. May 17, 2014. https://www.bbc.com/news/magazine-27442625.

Mason, Betsy, and Keith Axline. "A Brief History of Light." *Wired*. Dec. 25, 2000. https://www.wired.com/2008/12/gallery-lights/.

"The Most Toxic City in America." *Architectural Afterlife*. Jan. 15, 2019. https://architecturalafterlife.com/2019/01/15/the-most-toxic-city-in-america/.

Nace, Trevor. "This City Bench Absorbs More Air Pollution Than a Grove of Trees." *Forbes*. Mar. 20, 2018. https://www.forbes.com/sites/trevornace/2018/03/20/this-city-bench-absorbs-more-air-pollution-than-a-grove-of-trees/#c63b776b8d8f.

"Oil and Gas." *Open Secrets*. 2020. https://www.opensecrets.org/industries./recips. php?ind=E01++.

Peris, Eulalia. "Noise Pollution Is a Major Problem, Both for Human Health and the Environment." *European Environment Agency*. June 8, 2020. https://www.eea. europa.eu/articles/noise-pollution-is-a-major.

Potenza, Alessandra. "In 1952 London, 12,000 People Died from Smog—Here's Why That Matters Now." *The Verge*. Dec. 16, 2017. https://www.theverge. com/2017/12/16/16778604/london-great-smog-1952-death-in-the-air-pollu- tion-book-review-john-reginald-christie.

Semuels, Alana. "The Future Will Be Quiet." *The Atlantic*. Apr. 2016. https://www. theatlantic.com/magazine/archive/2016/04/the-future-will-be-quiet/471489/.

Shah, Vaidehi. "6 Water-Saving Innovations to Celebrate This World Water Day." *Eco-Business*. Mar. 22, 2017. https://www.eco-business.com/news/6-water-sav- ing-innovations-to-celebrate-this-world-water-day/.

Smith-Schoenwalder, Cecelia. "Malaysia to Ship Plastic Trash Back to the U.S., Other Origin Countries." *USA Today*. May 28, 2019. https://www.usnews.com/ news/world-report/articles/2019-05-28/malaysia-to-ship-plastic-trash-back-to- the-us-other-origin-countries.

Spinks, Rosie. "Could These Five Innovations Help Solve the Global Water Cri- sis?" *The Guardian*. Feb. 13, 2017. https://www.theguardian.com/global-devel- opment-professionals-network/2017/feb/13/global-water-crisis-innovation-solu- tion.

Sweeney, Kevin Z. *Prelude to the Dust Bowl: Droughts in the Nineteenth-Century Southern Plains*. Norman: University of Oklahoma Press, 2016.

"Vasily Dokuhaev and Soil Science." *SciHi Blog*. Oct. 26, 2016. http://scihi.org/ vasily-dokuchaev-and-soil-science/.

Wang, Jennifer, "Trump's Stock Portfolio: Big Oil, Big Banks and More Foreign Connections." *Forbes*. Nov. 29, 2016. https://www.forbes.com/sites/jennifer- wang/2016/11/29/trumps-stock-portfolio-big-oil-big-banks-and-more-foreign- connections/#63d3180f464e.

Wilcox, Christie. "Evolution: Out of the Sea." *Scientific American*. July 28, 2012. https://blogs.scientificamerican.com/science-sushi/evolution-out-of-the-sea/.

Yurk, Valerie. "Revealed: More Than 1,000 Metric Tons of Microplastics Rain Down on US Parks and Wilderness." *The Guardian*. June 11, 2020. https://www.the- guardian.com/environment/2020/jun/11/microplastics-us-national-parks-survey.

Zalzal, Kate S. "A Flammable Planet: Fire Finds Its Place in Earth History." *Earth*. Jan. 16, 2018. https://www.earthmagazine.org/article/flammable-planet-fire- finds-its-place-earth-history.

Websites

Earthjustice

www.earthjustice.org

Earthjustice began as the legal arm of the Sierra Club, one of the United States' oldest and most influential environmentalist organizations. The basic idea of Earthjustice is to support legal efforts to promote responsible ecological and environmental management and to oppose corporate and governmental exploitation of natural resources. Earthjustice has engaged in legal challenges over the provisions of the Clean Energy, Clean Air, and Clean Water acts and has been involved in a number of high-profile cases against petroleum companies in violation of national or international conventions on pollution and resource use. The organization also provides legal assistance and advocacy for local organizations seeking to use legal tools to prevent environmental exploitation and destruction.

Environmental Defense Fund (EDF)

www.edf.org

The Environmental Defense Fund (EDF) is a nonprofit environmental advocacy organization active in many different areas of environmental protection and rehabilitation. The EDF has programs addressing various kinds of pollution, including air pollution, water pollution, and the loss of species. The EDF focuses primarily on economic and market-based solutions to environmental issues and advocates for new federal and state laws addressing climate change, pollution, and environmental health.

The National Wildlife Federation (NWF)

www.nwf.org

The National Wildlife Federation (NWF) is one of the most influential environmental organizations in the realm of environmental protection and is also the largest private conservation organization in the United States. The NWF supports research and campaigns on a variety of different topics and has been involved in antipollution campaigns as part of their broader focus on protecting wildlife and the habitats necessary to enable the future survival of species. The NWF funds and supports educational efforts in schools and through television and print to increase environmental awareness. Some recent NWF campaigns have focused on oceanic plastic pollution and combating climate change.

The Natural Resources Defense Council (NRDC)

www.nrdc.org

The NRDC, founded in 1970, is a nonprofit advocacy and lobbyist organization dedicated to addressing global environmental destruction and degradation. Primary foci for the organization include climate change, water and air pollution, environmental issues and public health, and natural resource protection. The NRDC has contributed to key court cases involving environmental law and is one of the most influential organizations lobbying for federally protected parks and wilderness areas.

Ocean Conservancy

www.oceanconservancy.org

The Ocean Conservancy is a Washington, D.C.-based advocacy and activist organization focused specifically on marine conservation and protection. The Ocean Conservancy supports and publishes data and marketing materials on the importance of oceanic resources and promoting sustainability and responsible use of oceanic resources. Combating oceanic pollution, and especially plastic pollution, has become a central focus for the organization in the 2010s. In addition to providing, supporting, and funding research and public outreach campaigns, the Ocean Conservancy also organizes practical remediation efforts, such as beach and shallow water cleanup projects.

Sierra Club

www.sierraclub.org

The Sierra Club is one of the oldest environmentalist organizations in the United States, founded in 1892 by famed California environmentalist John Muir. The Sierra Club is involved in a variety of different environmentalist issues, providing funding, assistance, and advocacy for local and national researchers studying environmental issues and lobbying governmental organizations for stronger environmental protection laws. Among other issues, the Sierra Club supports campaigns to address air pollution, water pollution, soil pollution, and reducing greenhouse gases. In addition to environmental advocacy, the Sierra Club is also active in supporting local and national programs that help people engage with outdoor environments, through hiking, mountaineering, and river and oceanic recreational activities.

The Union of Concerned Scientists (UCS)

www.ucusa.org

The Union of Concerned Scientists is a nonprofit advocacy group founded in 1969 at the Massachusetts Institute of Technology (MIT). The organization attempts to collect and publicize scientific concerns regarding environmental and social justice issue. The UCS has funded research and reporting on pollution, climate change, resource degradation, and a number of other key issues. Among primary environmental goals of the UCS is to support expanding renewable energy and reducing greenhouse gases, issues that also overlap with the effort to control pollution in states and municipalities.

Index

DATE DUE

			PRINTED IN U.S.A.